ARKANA

The Year I

A key figure in the revolutionary field of dream and body work, and of psychological interventions in psychiatry, Arnold Mindell is the author of *Dreambody*, *Working with the Dreaming Body*, *River's Way*, *The Dreambody in Relationships*, *City Shadows* and *Working on Yourself Alone* (all published by Arkana), and *Coma*, *Key to Awakening*. He is an analyst in private practice, Founder of the Center for Process-Oriented Psychology, Zurich and Portland, and analyst and teacher both at this society and at the Jung Institute, Zurich. He has been a resident teacher at Esalen Institute, Big Sur, California.

Arnold Mindell

The Year I

Global Process Work

ARKANA

ARKANA

Published by the Penguin Group
27 Wrights Lane, London W8 5TZ, England
Viking Penguin Inc., 40 West 23rd Street, New York, New York 10010, USA
Penguin Books Australia Ltd, Ringwood, Victoria, Australia
Penguin Books Canada Ltd, 2801 John Street, Markham Ontario, Canada L3R 1B4
Penguin Books (NZ) Ltd, 182–190 Wairau Road, Auckland 10, New Zealand

Penguin Books Ltd, Registered Offices: Harmondsworth, Middlesex, England

First published 1989
1 3 5 7 9 10 8 6 4 2

Made and printed in Great Britain by
Richard Clay Ltd, Bungay, Suffolk
Filmset in Monophoto Bembo

Contents

Acknowledgements   vii

Insights, Dreams and Acknowledgements   1

I. Earth Problems

1   *Global Awareness*   9

    Collective consciousness; introduction to global process work – theory and practice

2   *Global Symptoms*   13

    Description of the world crisis situation; 'Global 2000'

3   *Solutions*   18

    Causal and behavioural solutions; global thinking; new paradigm shifts

II. Earth Fields

4   *Global Information Fields*   27

    Global information float; dreambody concepts; irrational planetary processes

5   *Global Dreambody Myths*   33

    Anthropos creation myths; the world as a dreaming body; global principles

6   *Global Suicide and Rebirth*   47

    Creation and annihilation myths; national history; community creation and suicide

7   *Earth Magic and Science*   55
    Morphic fields; relativity; nonlocality; Gaia principles; sys-
    tems theory and global mind
8   *Wake Up, Shiva*   63
    Perennial Indian philosophy; Shiva as a global sensory
    system; the meaning of consciousness

III. Global Process Work
9   *Fluctuation, Disturbance and Change*   73
    Perturbation; systems theory; racism; non–equilibrium pro-
    cess theory
10 *Group Process Structure*   82
    Segmentation; roles; polycephalous heads; ideology; net-
    work; awareness; garbage
11 *World Process Theatre*   96
    Group process interventions; dramatizing and unfolding
    fields
12 *War Games and Conflict Methods*   114
    War; altered–state training in fear and rage; large-group war
    process
13 *The Year I*   128
    World history and 'rights of man' revolutions integrated as
    interventions in modern times
14 *The Numinous Core*   136
    Review of assumptions; empirical group experience; one
    answer to where it is all going

    Notes   141
    Glossary   148
    Bibliography   152

Acknowledgements

The publishers make grateful acknowledgement to the following for permission to reproduce illustrations:

The Real World: Polar Projection Map of the World from the *Hammond New Practical World Atlas*, 1956. *The Tibetan Wheel of Becoming*: Victoria and Albert Museum. *Vedic God, Supreme Being*: The British Library. *Implicate Order in Hindu Cosmology*: British Library. *God as a Cosmic Architect*: Bild–Archiv der Österreichischen Nationalbibliothek, Vienna. *The World as a House of God*: Biblioteca Apostolica Vaticana, Rome. *Birth Moment in the Universe*: from Warren Kenton, *Astrology* (Thames & Hudson). *Divination Calculation Playing*: from Joseph Needham, *Science and Civilisation in China*, Vol. 3. *World Death and Rebirth in Japan*: from David Maclagan, *Creation Myths* (Thames & Hudson). *Vishnu-Krishna Manifesting Divine Form*: Collection Sven Gahlin, London. *Shiva's Dance*: Roloff Beny Archives, Vancouver. *Black Elk's Tribal Centre*: by kind permission of Hilda Neihardt Petri. *St Michael and the Devil*: Camera Press *Nuremberg Trial of War Criminals*: Hulton Picture Library. *Hungarian Uprising*: Hulton Picture Library.

Insights, Dreams and Acknowledgements

Global issues require coordinated, global, many-sided approaches. The process-oriented approach which I describe in this book has several characteristics that may extend modern theories of group dynamics or organizational development methods.

1. Unintended Behaviour

The solutions to all sorts of human problems are often hidden in our unintended behaviour, and in the unexpected events surrounding our groups and organizations, even when these events seem at first to be disturbances.

The gigantic problems facing us today require an approach that appreciates and values all of these unexpected events and that awakens us to the valuable secrets embedded in unintended and unexpected events. Criticizing ourselves for what we have done to our world may be helpful, but cannot change irreversible processes and rarely inspires us to react creatively or to raise the overall quality of our lives.

2. Global and Individual Work

We need to work with the whole organization or city and its environment as a single unit, process the tensions in its small subgroups, work with its couples, and work with each individual's internal conflicts. Working only on one of these levels is necessary but insufficient for assisting a global family to resolve its problems.

3. Practical and Spiritual Work

The spiritual component in any process-oriented view of human

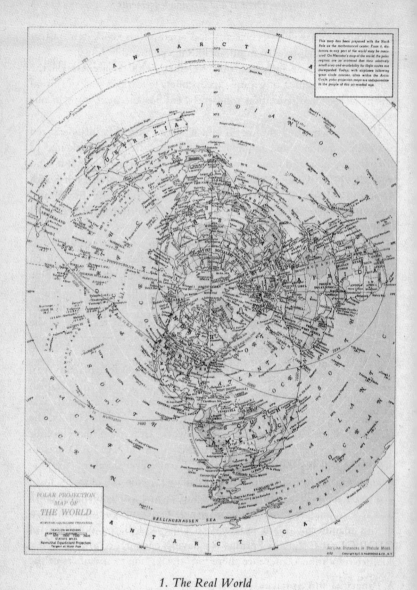

POLAR PROJECTION
MAP OF
THE WORLD

AZIMUTHAL EQUIDISTANT PROJECTION

SCALE ON MERIDIANS
0   500   1000   1500   2000
STATUTE MILES
Azimuthal Equidistant Projection
Tangent at North Pole

Air Line Distances in Statute Miles
Copyright by C. S. HAMMOND & CO., N.Y.

1. *The Real World*

behaviour compassionately accepts and attempts to work with all of our many possible states of mind, including anger and jealousy.

Wide experience indicates that together with awareness of the unintended behaviour of groups, an openness to various states of mind and to levels of organization frequently unfolds the next steps in our evolution.

The idea of treating the world as if it were a global family occurred to me in a dream about ten years ago. In that dream, I awakened to discover my new and huge family. New relatives were there. But who were they? Ten Chinese people, ten Russians, ten Africans, ten South Americans, Eskimos, Laplanders, central and northern Europeans, Australians, New Zealanders, Canadians and Americans. 'Welcome,' I said, and I woke up and decided to begin this book.

Shortly thereafter came two new dreams. In one, I was looking at the ocean and mountains, and there were great rocks in the sea. Each of the rocks had an eye! Powerful waves crashed up against these rocks and a wise dream teacher said, 'Find the equations which connect the human and the inorganic realms.' In the second dream, God brought me one of his patients and, as I peered fearfully at the enormous body of my new client, I recognized with a start that it was the world!

I am grateful to my dreams and especially thankful to many real people for their help and encouragement. I want to thank Amy Kaplan for her inspiration and for her many clarifying conversations. It was Barbara Croci who brought about the first dream. Ursula Hohler, the translator of the German edition of this work, cleared up many points. Thanks to Jan Dworkin for introducing me to UNCTAD and to other United Nations organizations. I am very thankful to Julie Diamond, Pearl Mindell and Dawn Menken for editorial help.

Thanks to Michael Murphy for having invited me to Esalen where I was able to examine successfully many of the conflict-resolution ideas of this manuscript. I am indebted to Janae and Barry Weinhold of CICRCL in Colorado Springs for having encouraged me to lead a conflict-resolution conference there introducing me to members of the US Air Force.

My students, classes and experiments at the Center for Process-Oriented Psychology in Zurich and at Esalen in Big Sur, California

2. The Dreaming World – The Tibetan Wheel of Becoming

have helped me to clarify and solidify my ideas. I was able to test, correct and amplify cross-cultural interventions of process work and conflict resolution in many cities around the world including Tel Aviv, Nairobi, Cape Town, Bombay, Tokyo and Honolulu.

I am infinitely grateful to many authors for introducing me to network and systems theory, to Malinowski's UNCTAD (United Nations Council for Trade and Development) theory and to Robert Muller's application of systems theory in the United Nations. I have tried to acknowledge all those authors from whom I have learned.

For help with organizational development and with group conflicts, contact the Process Work Center, Portland, Oregon.

Please see the glossary, page 148, for explanations of new, foreign or mythical terms.

Part I

Earth Problems

Chapter One

Global Awareness

The cross-cultural global theories and process-work interventions I present in this book have been tried and tested during the past ten years of conflict-resolution sessions with a variety of groups around the world. They enable informal groups and complex businesses to discover unexpected depths and centredness in community life by dealing not only with intended communication but also with the unintended, that is, the global atmosphere.

Having worked with a wide variety of people from the military, from new-age and spiritual groups, from organizations and states in conflict and from peace organizations, and having lived in different places in the world, I am shocked to discover that *global awareness is minimal.*

Global awareness, as I use it here, means having knowledge of our feelings and fantasies when alone and in groups; being aware of the reactions of other group members and network parts when representing our own ideas; and having awareness of our racist tendencies to gossip about, tyrannize or neglect those who are different from us. Most of us are at the beginning of global awareness in the senses just mentioned, even though we may pride ourselves on our ecological and political consciousness and our knowledge of the world's problems.

This lack of awareness is one reason why many of us feel like outsiders in our own world, why group interactions give us so much pain, and why we fantasize about leaving our bodies. How often do we feel like misanthropes, outsiders cast from the earth's heart, from its spiritual and familial nucleus? We barely realize that our own unconsciousness barricades us from others and from the rest of our world.

Yet we silently search for the excitement and richness of human connection, and often look in vain for the mysterious essence of

9

community. Our need for love and the freedom to be creative in groups remains a distant dream waiting for realization. One way to reach our spiritual and practical planetary goals is to reprocess our human garbage – the emotional tension we throw into the atmosphere, the unresolvable, impossible, and forbidden fantasies about ourselves and others that we leave for the next generation to clean up. When recycled and processed, this tension brings us the missing enlightenment and altered states which facilitate the solutions to our problems.

The people who fought for and won the 'rights of man' during the French Revolution were certainly justified in marking the success of 1792 as the **Year I**. We are still fighting today, not only for the right and freedom to self-determination, but for the awareness that all of our parts and all of the different roles in the world are necessary for planetary survival.

This book assumes that, once again, today is the Year I. We are again in the midst of a revolution, this time with our own awareness. This work contributes to the revolution by developing theories and methods which support the rights of all human beings and group parts to work with the human network which creates our world. I present a many-levelled, process-oriented way of understanding and working with planetary processes and conflicts in individuals, in relationships, and in small and large groups.

Those of us worried about the world situation need methods which

i. work rapidly, are diverse and many-levelled

ii. value and connect known psychological, ecological, spiritual and behavioural approaches with conflict-resolution methods for small and large groups

iii. deal with the dangers of emotional escalations leading to war and recognize the potential meaning in anger

iv. are cross-cultural and have been tested

v. allow for divergent opinions and positions on collective events.

Most of us sense that we must increase our level of individual and group awareness if our planet is to survive its problems. Ecological, women's, and civil rights movements have made us realize that our basic problems lie deeper than the issues at hand. We need to learn how to address our differences. Today, groups and movements must not only accomplish tasks but, like the individuals within these groups, must model the essence which gives them life.

To expedite this awareness, the first part of the book is devoted to the earth's problems and attempted solutions. The second part shows how global myths, patterns and ideologies are like planetary dreams and organize the behaviour of groups, networks and nations, and how these collective dreams organize difficult planetary processes. The third section of the book integrates network and systems theory with process-oriented thinking (Mindell, *River's Way*), and develops an anthropomorphic field theory. Planetary process work is applied in the last section to conflict resolution in small and large groups and to military and economic difficulties faced by the United Nations.

I attempt to show how global processes are organized by a dream-like field, a troubled sea of projections, feelings and ecological confusion, floating between both individuals and groups, confusing communication and creating war. When properly recycled, this 'information float' creates the harmony and wholeness we are looking for. Yet when unprocessed, it disturbs both individual and group and creates our worst problems. This phenomenon goes by many names: information float, morphic collective unconscious, the global atmosphere. Whatever its name, its powerful emanations permeate our lives, healing and destroying. When unused, it becomes a festering, global-information cloud, an explosive dump responsible for nightmarish planetary problems.

Though we speak of rapid change and the coming of a new age, we are today on the verge of planetary extinction. We are still burdened by exactly the same unsolved emotional problems which caused our earliest ancestors to murder one another. As we approach the end of the twentieth century, we hear daily about industrial and chemical spills, dying forests, poisoned food, water and air, and the threat of nuclear war. These problems threaten the very existence of the earth, and affect distant parts of the world we thought would never touch us.

None of us realizes the power of our own potential global awareness.

That is why we project it upon the leaders of our groups, expecting them to create the world we need instead of developing our own ability to deal with ourselves and our groups. We are surprised that the 'experts' who were going to save us also live in the same troubled field as we do and are, as a result, as unknowing as we.

Modern physics warns us that our universe is post-Einsteinian or, in other words, a space with 'no localities', where everything is instantly connected and where everyone's thoughts and feelings intermingle, creating a world in which hiding is impossible; we cannot avoid one another. Ecology needs an extended meaning. In the Year I, we realize that nothing, not even fantasies, feelings or thoughts, can be thrown away because they no longer have anywhere to go.

Chapter Two

Global Symptoms

The earth suffers from a number of ecological and political problems threatening its survival. Since 1945, we have been living in more or less constant fear of a nuclear catastrophe, either the result of a radioactive leak from a power plant or of a political conflict escalating into an atomic nightmare. Einstein said in 1946, 'The unleashed power of the atom has changed everything save our modes of thinking, and thus we drift towards unparalleled catastrophe.'[1]

Is the solution to this impending explosion the increase or reduction of nuclear arms? Decreasing or increasing nuclear arms may momentarily reduce the threat of war, but it does not deal with the impulse behind such weapons, namely, the drive for self-expression and power as a protection against insecurity and conflict.

What outer factors make a country feel powerful? At present, a strong national defence, successful participation in world trade and financing, and autonomy seem to make a country feel powerful. But is this attainable today? There are indications that even the superpowers have already reached their peak in terms of wealth and independence. And in its attempt to become powerful and enter the Western trade race, the Third World faces a future with even more problems than at present.

Our present militaristic and economic solutions do not pacify our imagination; we still believe that the neighbouring countries want blood. Conflict, or at least tension, is here to stay, and with it, the desire for and challenge of war. Can we transform aggression and insecurity into relationship? We have created a United Nations through our global efforts, giving us symptomatic relief, but lacking true success. In the haste to paste the world together, this organization and others like it may even be creating as much conflict as peace. I will discuss in Chapters 11 and 13 how to develop a global perspective, how to focus simultaneously on the overall picture and on the individual nations.

But the danger of war and the nuclear threat are only two of many symptoms contributing to a syndrome of a world in trouble. The United States Government Council on Environmental Quality's report on the state of the world, 'Global 2000', indicates that the planet in the 1980s suffers from overpopulation, poverty, energy shortages, malnutrition and environmental pollution.[2] For the sake of completeness, I would like briefly to review some of the council's conclusions:

a. **The Population Bomb**

It took humankind over a million years to reach a population of one billion by the year 1800. Today, 189 years later, we number almost five billion. Ten billion is the 'maximum that an intensively managed world might hope to support with some degree of comfort'. At the present rate of growth, this number will be reached by the year 2030. Over 90 per cent of the population growth occurs in the less-developed countries. By the year 2000, 80 per cent of the world's population will be packed into these countries.

b. **Poverty**

Over half the world, 2.5 billion people, now live on less than $500 a year. Eight hundred million people lack adequate housing or shelter, and 10 million suffer from preventable blindness.

c. **Food**

This year alone, 15 to 20 million people will die of malnutrition, while 600 million are undernourished.

d. **Energy**

We have not yet been forced, due to non-renewable energy sources such as wood, coal, oil, gas, etc., to change our energy usage to solar, wind or hydroelectric power. Yet our resources are dwindling quickly, and our lack of concern about energy cannot continue much longer. In underdeveloped countries energy sources are so scarce that energy research and development diverts money from food, education and medicine.

e. Environment

Virtually every aspect of the earth's ecosystem and resource base is polluted and disturbed by the population's waste products. Arable land, drinking water, deserts, the atmosphere, the climate, forests and vegetation are disturbed by the industrial world.

f. Agriculture

Farmland is pushed to its production limits and beyond. Soil depletion is one of the results. Erosion, nutrient loss, pollution and water shortages reduce productivity, destroy farmland, and increase the percentage of desert. It is predicted that forests may be largely depleted by early in the next century.

g. Atmosphere and Climate

Atmospheric pollution, urban air pollution, and rising carbon-dioxide concentrations combine to form what 'Global 2000' calls a 'chemical leprosy . . . eating into the face of North America and Europe'. This chemical legacy creates, among other problems, 'acid rain', which occurs when sulphur-dioxide and nitrogen-oxide emissions combine with atmospheric water vapour to form acid.

Present Difficulties

I stress these difficult symptoms instead of lauding global progress in technology and communications in order to bridge the gap between our numbed awareness of the global dangers and our interest in changing them.

As Rifkin states:

> There are accidents at nuclear power plants, shootouts in gas station lines over fuel allocations, the doubling and tripling of inflation figures, the steady loss of productivity and jobs, increased danger of thermonuclear war . . .

> . . . garbage and pollution are piling up in every quarter . . . seeping into our rivers, and lingering in our air. Our eyes burn, our skin discolours, our lungs collapse . . .

> . . . Everywhere we go we find ourselves waiting in lines or pushed into corners. We are bogged down, the society is bogged down . . . [3]

Fritjof Capra, Hazel Henderson and others demonstrate that the experts in various fields can no longer deal with the urgent problems which have arisen in their areas of expertise.[4] Economists are unable to deal with inflation; oncologists are confused about the causes of cancer; psychiatrists are mystified by schizophrenia; police are helpless in the face of criminal behaviour; and national governments are powerless in the face of terrorism. It seems as if the era of finding monocausal solutions to problems is over. We no longer live in a time in which a simple, single solution can solve a large group problem.

The Dream Field of the Earth

Economists, environmentalists, politicians and futurists reformulate these problems in anthropomorphic terms. Just as we notice that certain ways of behaving sicken our personal bodies, we also see that the earth is no longer well. Our planet's population growth is likened to a cancerous tumour, growing out of control. Much of humankind is poor and starving; our planet's energy resources are fatigued, in some cases, exhausted. The state of our environment, the earth's surface, atmosphere and climate show a planet in poor physical condition.

But the above anthropomorphic tendency is only just beginning. When I look at the 'Global 2000' report, I can see a possible reason for the population explosion: there are simply not enough real, conscious human beings who do as they say! Instead of creating more consciousness, we unconsciously try to create more people.

I have seen widespread economic poverty, but even more widespread human undernourishment: individuals and groups for whom no one has time. Many of us are hungry; all of us spiritually impoverished. We are becoming aware of the global energy crisis, but we forget that many of us no longer have the vitality to continue living on this planet. Our air is polluted to the danger point, but the atmosphere between us has been catastrophic for centuries. It seems as if the physical body of the world may finally awaken us to the dream-like problems making us ill.

How sick are we? Global symptoms may be indications that our planetary dreambody, like a human dreambody, is trying to bring forth a new vision. Our present body is running out of energy and resources – it is bulging at the seams. While we fervently apply first aid to the worst of our wounds, something is dreaming that this is the end of an era, the end of an old human form.

Chapter Three

Solutions

In analytical circles it used to be customary to think of individuation as a task of the second half of life, one marked by increased interest in the world at large. Today, however, so many people are becoming actively involved in world processes that this is no longer the case. Now, having travelled so much in different parts of the world, people of all ages, everywhere, are seeing the world situation as one of their personal problems.

Numerous factors interact to awaken us to the existence of the world's problems. The most apparent development is in communications. The launching of the communication satellite Sputnik in 1957 was, in a way, the beginning of the communication age. The launching of the satellite was a quantum jump in sending long-distance messages. When John F. Kennedy was shot, for example, a reporter at his typewriter in Dallas, just across the street from where the President was killed, first got word of the assassination by satellite report through his radio. Such rapid long-distance communication makes the world smaller and its events more accessible to us.

The world's problems interest and involve us more immediately. Until now it was chiefly politicians, military strategists, media reporters, religious leaders, business people and economists who were involved in the world situation. Everyone tried to solve their problems according to their particular paradigm. Today, such monocausal solutions, which come from isolated systems, continue to be important steps in working on global processes, but they rarely meet with long-term results. Today, individuation must include global awareness and systemic thinking.

For the purpose of discussion, the present methods and psychology for dealing with world problems may be generalized and categorized

as: (1) ignoring problems, (2) trying causal solutions, (3) trying behavioural modification, and (4) using a paradigm shift to global
thinking.

1. Ignoring Problems

Most of us faced with the problems of our earth close our ears and
eyes. We secretly believe that the world is full of self-healing magic.
When the city becomes too much for us we retreat, like true nature
lovers, to the woods and forget it. We develop a numbness when faced
with a crowded bus, apathy when asked how to deal with war, and an
inferiority complex when we read about terrorist attacks.

We are not really unconscious, we simply want to avoid problems.
And mostly we are afraid. We just do not know how to handle a tense
conflict with a neighbour, and when it comes to global conflicts and
the grey smog of daily life, we collapse.

2. Trying Causal Solutions

When problems become severe enough to break through our numbness, we turn to the experts in given fields to repair the difficulty, by
treating the symptoms. 'Tell us what to do!' we demand. When
unemployment makes us poor, when inflation rises too much, we turn
to our government economists or put our hopes in the social security
system. When there is a shortage of gas, we place our confidence in
atomic reactors, or attempt to use less energy. When traffic forms a
bottleneck on the Walensee in Switzerland, we make the autobahn
larger, inadvertently creating traffic jams in Zurich.

Our first step in saving our planet is necessarily monocausal first aid:
we seek to improve environmental conditions and protect the planet
by cleaning the lakes; forbidding people to throw away toxic wastes;
encouraging the use of renewable fuels; and by plugging up reactor
leaks. Yet our causal methods are disturbed by the unavoidable fact
that corrections to problems create more problems and more entropy.[1]
For example, in order to use solar energy, we have to use the

environment as a heat reservoir and this, in turn, creates waste products. All attempts to save one resource use more of another resource.

3. Trying Behavioural Modification

Therefore, some experts say, the best way to decrease planetary destruction is to do less: 'small is beautiful' is their motto. Such recommendations border on behavioural modification. We are told to change our behaviour. But something inhibits us from changing our behaviour. Even in the face of death, there is an incomprehensible force which refuses to let us change. We even raise the speed limits again, after lowering them to save fuel!

We are told that this is due to our egotism, our 'skin encapsulated egos', our lack of consideration for others. We already suspected this, but knowing does not help. We use more electricity now than ever before. Being told we are naughty also does not help.

We demonstrate against bombs, regulate nuclear power plants to make them safer, freeze the arms race, fix the broken pipe responsible for pollution, and drive more slowly. Our behavioural attempts are causal attempts to stop us from doing what we are doing and to change our nature. We use less energy, buy less tin foil, become less greedy, stop our jealousy, raise our consciousness, and try to feel more for others and for the planet.

Why don't we change? Could there possibly be something useful in our deviant behaviour? Why do we need to buy destructive materials? Why can't we inhibit our jealousy and greed? Do we need, for some reason, to maintain our egotism? Why do we love creating instruments which destroy ourselves and the environment? It could be that greed, jealousy, hatred and competition, when processed, bring us closer to our fellow human beings.[2] Love is not the only connecting force between people. In an effort to follow ancient religions or be new-age people, we equate enlightenment with harmony, stability and equilibrium. But equilibrium and harmony are only momentary states. When jealousy is processed with awareness, it turns into personal growth.

What shall we do with our aggression if we forbid it in our personal life? If we repress it, it goes into the body. Since our world sanctifies national conflict, much of our aggression finally overflows into our interest, fascination and investment in war. Without our being aware of it, our anger gets channelled into national conflict, which is not so close to home. War becomes a way for us to have our anger at a distance, impersonally. Our enemies abroad know very well that we are not as nice as we act at home.

Unprocessed information and experience poison the body and the environment. Just as there is an ecology of the physical planet, there is also a psycho-ecology. Throw out information and it festers and destroys. We have to learn to use our base states by processing them. A process-oriented view understands greed, jealousy, pride, ambition and egotism as momentary states whose meaning can be discovered only by unfolding them.[3]

4. Using Global Thinking

The philosophy behind behavioural modification imagines a pre-Copernican world in which the earth is the centre of the solar system and the individual ego is the centre of the universe. In the new paradigm shift, we are advised to 'think globally but act locally', in contrast to thinking only of ourselves.[4] The new age is a systems age. We are being taught to realize that we are whole in ourselves, and also that we are part of a larger whole whose existence depends upon us.

This book tries to contribute to the means of accomplishing the shifting paradigms. But let's look more closely at two stumbling blocks to the present paradigm of 'thinking globally'.

i. Egotism: we are and have been too egotistical, and

ii. Entropy: we are wasteful, wanting more without considering what we are wasting.

How do we deal with egotism and the resulting low synergy and high entropy which inhibit global thinking?

i. **Egotism**

Egotism is not a fault but a fact. In the process view, egotism is not a defect but a sign that the person or group is insecure about their identity. Criticizing egotism does not change things. The egotist needs support as well as insight! In fact, the egotist lets go of the ego too easily. The egotist actually needs to stick up for his or her viewpoint so that a true debate and learning process can ensue. We cannot think of others before remembering ourselves. Being self-centred is a symptom of not appreciating one's own viewpoint. Egotism persists if its view is not supported.

ii. **Entropy**

The entropy paradigm in physics is based upon the physicist's concept of closed systems with boundaries.[5] Telepathic and psychokinetic events indicate, however, that the mind is not necessarily bound to the brain, and our energy sometimes appears to be coupled in a way which confounds the classical concept of physical boundaries.

An increase in entropy in a bounded system assumes that the total energy becomes less available to the observer for work. In a human system, however, apparently lost, unconscious information and entropic behaviour can be accessed, with awareness, to create new forms of behaviour. We are capable of delving into the nature of our illnesses and rediscovering lost information and meaning there.

The entropy concept in physics, as it now stands, does not include human awareness. When Maxwell developed the entropy idea, he said that it could be reversed if there were a little person, a demon, known today as the Maxwellian Demon, who lived inside the system and who could follow its inner workings, with awareness. He imagined something like the picture opposite.

The normal course of events in the closed system assumes, of course, that there is no one in there, no consciousness that can operate the door separating compartments, no one who can intervene in the relationship between parts.

The reality of this lack of consciousness in matter might be debated, but my experience with tension in groups leads me to believe that

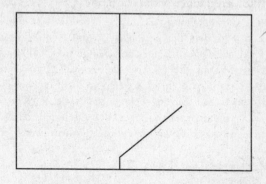

Closed System with the Demon of Consciousness

there is rarely anyone present who consciously and usefully intervenes in troubled relationships. Hence, entropy reigns in the sense of losing available energy and information. In other words, if some form of consciousness is present in the troubled planetary systems we live in, then the global degeneration and misery predicted by the second law might be reversed. *But*, how many of us are conscious, especially when caught in the midst of our own family system, groups and large national problems! The second law remains true as long as there is no one at 'home', so to speak, no one who is awake enough to process emotions, use tensions and reduce pain.

Hence, the entropy hypothesis is applicable only to those situations lacking human awareness. Where there is global awareness, that is, knowledge about intervening on many different cultural levels at once (a method I will discuss in Chapters 10 and 11) there is a minimal amount of entropy and a maximum amount of transformation, community synergy and enjoyment.

Thus, the beginning of a new paradigm shift in thinking globally is to value the viewpoint of the egotist and the system awareness of the process worker. Global thinking should consider both monocausal and long-term system solutions, value nationalism as well as universality, and become aware of both the present and the eternal. Global awareness becomes most important when we are locked into closed emotional systems. There is the place for the Maxwellian Demon; there consciousness can make a great difference in our future.

Part II

Earth Fields

Chapter Four

Global Information Fields

Why is it that the ailing human body does not always respond to causal medical treatment? One answer is that the body is not only a Newtonian machine but a 'dreambody', a body with a dream field around it, organizing experiences which cannot be changed by antibiotics.

In this chapter I will show that the same principle holds for the earth as well. The ailing earth often fails to respond well to causal, local treatments because causal solutions do not take sufficient account of the earth's global nature, its information network, its dreaming and mythical core. In this and the following chapters we shall study these special information field effects.

The Global Mind in the Individual

Obviously, one of the main reasons why we are so concerned with our planet is because it is suffering so severely. But this is not the only reason. The threat of world war has been present for a long time. And there have always been those who fantasized at one time or another that the world would come to an apocalyptic end, through an evil god or through the gods destroying themselves.

There are many reasons for the universal change in attitudes towards the planet. One is simply that it is an inner characteristic of our times. A second is the outer ecological problems. A third is the sudden growth of interest in transpersonal, holistic and shamanistic psychologies, and our increased interest in belief systems, astronomy and modern physics that suggests a worldwide change in our psychological constitution. Our awareness is opening up and becoming more global.

We are beginning to realize what our tribal nomadic sisters and brothers have always said: the world is a part of us and behaves as if it were one of our senses!

We are creating psychologies which deal with our spiritual selves; we are opening up to our deaths and afterlives; and we are attempting to send messages to aliens on other planets in part because our own global nature is awakening.[1]

Information Aspects of the Global Mind

The global aspect of our collective mind possesses some of the following characteristics. It focuses not only upon details, but also upon interconnections, couplings, and networks of events. It is able to look at the same event from various viewpoints and levels. It changes one part with an awareness of other parts, and understands the world as a field or network of information. According to a consensus of opinion, we have changed from an industrial world to one resembling a huge information-processing community.[2]

Eighty-five per cent of all the jobs in the United States are related to the processing of information.[3] The rest of the world is quickly following suit. Secretaries, psychologists, doctors, teachers and lawyers are, from this new point of view, processors of information. And many other jobs, although not exclusively processing information, deal with information, at least in part.

This means that we store and retrieve information technically, we use computers and satellites, and we do more networking with one another than ever before. It means that we buy and sell information, and that facts and knowledge are important to us. It means that the way we think is becoming as important to us as the way in which we produce things.

The Information Dreambody Field

In this and the next few chapters I will be collecting ideas from mythology, modern physics, religion, sociology, psychology and systems theory which indicate that our world is a combination of physical objects and dream-like patterns, or fields, of information. The new information description of the Western world in the early 1980s is a great aid in conceptualizing a global field as having memory, collective archetypal patterns, and the capacity to influence thinking, behaviour and environmental events.

In the past, causally inexplicable and synchronistic events were attributed to God, mere accident, or karmic and magical influence. Today, irrational body problems and symptoms can be understood through dreambody considerations, through the idea that body experiences are organized by the overall process of individuation which can be seen in the dreams of an individual.[4]

Global ecological and social events which cannot fully be explained by causal reasoning, such as the same discovery happening simultaneously in various parts of the world, can be understood as manifestations of archetypal patterns of Jung's collective unconscious or of Rupert Sheldrake's morphic fields.[5] According to these ideas, everything, from our personal problems to collective difficulties, such as stock market crashes, is touched and created by the dream-like atmosphere in which we live. Unusual events in the animal kingdom, such as the sudden tendency of a given bird species to commit suicide, can be understood (by Jung) as a meaningful coincidence determining the fate of the flock or (by Sheldrake) as an example of 'morphic resonance' between members of the same groups.[6]

The dreambody idea expresses the empirical side of Sheldrake's morphic field and Jung's collective unconscious. We can notice how dreams and information of which we are unconscious (such as myths, beliefs, jealousies and other affects) organize our physical experiences, and create and complicate the atmosphere surrounding our relationships by forcing us to communicate in unintended ways.[7] I will show in Chapters 9 and 10 how the future of our small groups depends upon these dreams and unconscious collective patterns.[8]

I shall be showing how these dream fields not only organize personal and small group processes, but acausal, inexplicable global situations as well. We shall need such field theories and special methods when working with events not amenable to current solutions, such as the death of our trees and terrorist attacks.

Reducing the Information Float

A new awareness of information will aid us in understanding the details of ordinary communication problems. We are learning only now how we tend to pick up certain messages and neglect others. Information which is not picked up or which is blocked 'floats' like a fog of uncertainty between people. One of the goals of psychology is to study this information float, to differentiate intended from unconscious or unintended messages, and to discover how to decipher all human messages so that they may enrich, instead of confuse, relationships.

Information technology and psychology have at least one purpose in common: to reduce the 'float' and decrease the collective unconsciousness. Technology tries to reduce the float by reducing the time taken between the sending and the receiving of a message. Soon our mail systems will be organized so that we can all write a letter directly through a home computer to another home computer, virtually reducing the float time to zero.

Psychology, too, tries to reduce the time needed between sending and receiving a message. Understanding our dreams and body experiences makes us feel more whole. Understanding one another deepens relationships. In fact, the closer we get to our dreams and to one another, the less we can identify who sends and who receives information, as both the receiver and sender become joint participants in creating new experiences and information.

This 'floating information' arises from many different sources:

1. Xenophobia: the message would be too new or too threatening to our ordinary mind
2. Channel Incongruity: the message comes in a way or channel or language with which we are not familiar
3. Source Unrelatedness: we cannot relate to the source enough to encourage it to send clearer messages.

In our individual lives, we ignore dreams and body experiences which threaten our present identities. We focus on messages we can see or hear, and rarely pick up information coming in body channels or through relationships. We have very little connection with our many different communication capacities.

Information Float in a Group

Groups behave similarly. Thus a group of religious idealists will feel threatened by anyone who mentions egotism. A new-age group will ignore criticism which implies that they are stuck in the medieval period. We are all xenophobic. We throw out information and create an ecological mess by rejecting threatening facts. The float finally clogs up the atmosphere and ruins the group, the relationships within it and those with other organizations.

Just as the individual has many channels of expression, a group, too, uses various channels to express itself. If a group focuses only on what is being discussed, it will miss information coming from other channels, such as its movements or feelings expressed outside the group. The disturber of the group, the outside world, or the dreams of its members are pieces of information which then appear in unused channels, information a group rarely picks up. Channel incongruity creates an information float or dump, like a garbage dump, which festers if it is not recycled.

I shall show later in this book how we can develop methods of approaching the rejected and unknown sources of new information, how we can befriend the disturber, work with dreams, and pick up unintended information.

Consider, for example, the information float at the United Nations Conference on Trade and Development (UNCTAD) on Third World problems. There has long been a paralysing stalemate between Third World countries, the so-called Group of 77, and the North. The blocked negotiations between the North and the South help to create a precarious economic and political situation.

The South feels weak and disunified, while the North feels obligated to give, though not necessarily wanting to.[9] This dangerous situation is an example of an apparently logical economic problem which is disturbed by an information float, a dreambody field. What is the field exactly? It is only partly composed of the money problems, the intended issues at hand.

This information field is jammed full of emotional problems, unintended issues waiting to be processed. If you think of the Third World as a person, then we can imagine this person to be angry at the

North for its past policies of colonialism and slavery. Economics cannot be separated from feelings.

The xenophobic emotional terror, the channel incongruity of a group focused on logical expression yet plagued by emotions, and the source unrelatedness which represses issues such as colonialism all create a field of ignorance, vengeance and conflict; this field needs to be processed before any solution can help.

But our technical and psychological abilities at processing information have not yet reached the point where we can:

a. differentiate intended from unintended messages
b. relate to the sources of the information float
c. reduce the float and create new communication bonds.

Thus, the birth of the information planet and the promise it holds for the future is a possible, but as yet still mythical dream trying to happen. And until it does, we will have to live in the midst of a cloud, an information float, a collective unconsciousness which influences us in apparently mysterious ways. The world is a massive mind dreaming away, full of jewels hidden in the garbage waiting to be recycled.

Chapter Five

Global Dreambody Myths

The modern view of the world as an information network of interconnecting links, and of the planet as a thinking organism is not new, but has its roots in early myths, which portray the cosmos as a living being, a gigantic anthropos in which we all live. In this chapter I shall connect these ancient anthropos myths to modern scientific theories.

Anthropomorphic representations of the earth appear all over the world. In the typical anthropos myths of ancient civilizations, the universe is depicted as an immense god that created itself, human beings and the environment. For example, in Native American legends, the earth is described as a being, which is sore and suffering from the white people's insensitivity. In India, as well, the earth is the Vedic god, Indras, an immense living hologram whose parts mirror the pattern of the whole. He wears a necklace in which every bead is a different world.

In the Hindu cosmogony, this supreme being creates all the worlds (see Picture 3). 'From every hair of his body a world is suspended, and each world undergoes a certain number of dissolutions and renovations.'[1] In Picture 3 we see that each of us is one of his 'hairs'; we are outgrowths of the mind of a self-organizing being. We can see that the morphic fields of the collective unconscious have their ancient prefigurations here.

Just as whole worlds are in his beads, or hairs, many world religions imagine the world to be contained in a grain of dust. To use Bohm's terminology, the inner order of the universe is represented as a sort of 'implicate' pattern that expresses itself in the 'explicate' manifestations.[2] Picture 4 depicts a world as the uppermost level of existence, supported by an 'implicate' order, symbolized by snakes, elephants and, finally, Vishnu himself in the depths of the universe. Beneath our animal or instinctive behaviour lies a human-like god.

3. Vedic Supreme God

Zukav, an interpreter of modern physics, claims that the newfound wholeness in the sciences is really one of the prime aspects of our universe. He calls this wholeness the earth mother, Kali, whom the Hindus love and must honour. 'The Wu Li Masters know that the physicists are doing more than "discovering the endless diversity of nature". They are dancing with Kali, the Divine mother of Hindu mythology.'[3] The anthropos, a divine human being representing our universe, is a symbol for the deity that fascinates physicists in their quantum field theories about the physical world.

4. Implicate Order in Hindu Cosmology

The Anthropic Principle

We perceive the universe through a mixture of inner myths and outer technical instruments. Thus, it is not surprising that we find anthropomorphic views of the universe in both physics and mythology. Research in astronomy also leads us today to believe that we can observe only the aspect of the world around us which created life.

According to George Gale's 'Anthropic Principle', astronomers must adopt a new way of thinking.[4] When astronomers study the universe, they now realize that they cannot objectively deduce information about the beginning of the universe because the beginning conditions of the universe are unknowable and therefore unprovable. Gale argues that not only is the beginning speculative and non-reproducible, but the information we have at present is insufficient to deduce the beginning. The reason for this is what he calls the 'anthropic principle'.

Since the universe we observe now is the one which supports life on earth, we can only see a life-producing universe and cannot imagine other possibilities. As part of the universe, part of the anthropos under observation, we are not objective. Since we are studying ourselves, we cannot know whether there were earlier universes in which life was impossible. We see only that anthropos of which we are now part. In studying ourselves, we can speak of self-discovery but nothing else.

The Creation of the Anthropos

Many people have imagined the world to be an anthropos who dreamed himself and the world into being. An Alaskan tale tells us that the first living being was 'Father Raven'.

> He was not an ordinary bird but a holy life-power which was in everything which existed in this world in which we now live . . . But he, too, began in the shape of a human being . . .
> . . . He sat crouching in the darkness when he suddenly awoke to consciousness and discovered himself.[5]

Here, Father Raven is described as the world mind and the world itself. He is the first human being and also the spirit of the earth which he created. This global spirit or mind brings himself suddenly to consciousness by discovering himself. This is an ancient version of the recent belief in modern astronomy that the world was created with a 'big bang'.

We cannot be certain if the universe was created by Father Raven's awakening, but we can see that he is still trying to awaken today. All of us are beginning to realize that we do dream the world into being with our ideals and unconscious beliefs. Our earth is really only on the verge of discovering its own mind, its very existence! Until now, the anthropos did not know that it was a whole. Our world has not had to behave as a unity; it has been split into parts, which have hated and loved, lived in peace and died in war with one another. I guess if Father Raven sits in the darkness long enough, he will awaken in each of us. What we call global consciousness is the awakening of Father Raven.

According to the Uitoto Indians of Columbia, our universe was dreamed up and projected from the great spirit that lives in everything.

> First there is the world, the soundless sound, the beginning of nothingness. From this non-existence, the Father, the Cosmic Body, appears as a pure being. He is the creator. Those who have dreamed into Cosmic dimensions have been creators of the great systems . . . out of his own Being, he maintains the illusion and ties it to a dream, presses the magical substance [which is consciousness] to the illusion and the world comes into existence. It is a reality: he is able to sit down on his own earth.[6]

The experience of the world as a dream of a cosmic parental figure is often felt by us all. When we go out at sundown, into the desert, the woods or the sea, we are awed by the power and vastness of the environment. In spite of our scientific understanding of nature, the overwhelming beauty and majesty of drifting clouds and colourful lakes still convey the feeling that the earth was dreamed up and created by a numinous power.

We experience the earth as a creative spirit when synchronicities happen, when a dream connects to a real event. We also experience this spirit power in relationships when something seems to make our partners behave like our most difficult dream figures![7] Don Juan, the Yaqui shaman, who is connected to the earth's spirit, tells Castaneda that the world is his hunting ground and every bit of it is meant to be used.[8] Don Juan means that the world is a dream, a spirit waiting to be discovered.

The North American Zuni myth of creation tells us that Awonawilona, a prefiguration of our sun, was

> alone . . . [He] conceived in himself the thought, and the thought took shape and got out into space and through this it stepped out into the void, into outer space, and from them came nebulae of

growth and mist, full of power of growth. After the mist and nebulae came up, Awonawilona changed himself through his knowledge into another shape and became the sun, who is our father and who enlightens everything and fills everything with light, and the nebulae condensed and sank down and became water and thus the sea came into existence.[9]

The World as a Dreaming Body

Awonawilona is thus the power of thought, the sun and our universe. Awonawilona enlightens us about new things; he creates our world. The sun is our awareness. The brighter we become, the more we create and the more responsibility we have to take for our creations, for the world the way it is. Fantasies and dreams, according to this Zuni tale, have a tendency to realize themselves!

M. Eliade, reporting on ancient beliefs, formulates this dreaming power differently. 'The world that surrounds us . . . [has] an extraterrestrial archetype . . . a "double" existing on a higher cosmic level.'[10] In other words, the world is a real body whose physical behaviour is partly patterned by dreams. In cosmological terms, we could say that the earth is a dreaming body, organized by divine patterns.

These myths picture the earth as a living body with a dreaming mind. It is not just an electrical nervous system, but a dreaming system, and the events and conflicts here on earth are manifestations of its dream.

Divine Plans

The concept of a global body reflecting divine dreams is also found in European alchemy. The alchemist, Gerhard Dorn, had a theory of the '*unus mundus*' – the one world – which stated that the known world is designed by divine female powers, the dreams of a god or of a spirit. According to Von Franz,

The '*unus mundus*' is a medieval theological concept which holds that when God created the world he naturally first made a plan, like a good architect, a model of the cosmos . . . This '*unus mundus*' is not the cosmos as it exists now, but an idea in God's psyche or mind, the plan which God proceeds to realize, as an architect follows his plan for the building of a house.[11]

In Picture 5 we see the '*unus mundus*' as the global anthropos dreaming and planning reality. In Dorn's mind, this plan is feminine, wise and motherly. The world is a female idea, a concept of relatedness, a dream still trying to happen. For the medieval Church, the world itself was Christ, the house of God (see Picture 6). The most prominent figure in that picture is the Church as the mystical body of Christ, which contains, as in many medieval maps, the geography of the world.

The Human Being and the Universe

Krishna teaches in the *Bhagavad-gita* that the entire world resembles a human being. According to Buddhism, Buddha is in every particle of dust in this world. Medieval Europe saw the planetary constellations of the universe in the human body, as an incarnation of a particular moment in time.

In Picture 7 we see that every human experience is a birth, reflecting the astral constellations of a given moment. According to astrology, our own birth is the manifestation of a particular moment of the universe. Of this, the romantic poet Novalis says,

> The world is the Macro-anthropos, there is a world-mind
> just as there is a world-soul. The soul must become mind;
> the body must become world.[12]

Our personal bodies and dreams are channels of global potentials; we are manifestations of a universal dream and body.

The Tao of the Global Mind

These astrological concepts, as well as the idea of God's anima and Christ's appearance as the divine Logos of our world, imply that the field structure we live in is highly ordered by a human-like mind. The

5. God, the Cosmic Architect

6. *The World as a House of God*

7. *Moment of Birth in the Universe*

Chinese idea of the Tao is another such field concept. The Tao is the way in which individuals perceive or receive this global field. It is interesting to note that the Chinese concept of a field is not personified in the form of gods, but apprehended as a primitive mathematical

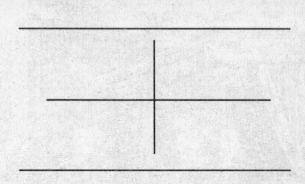

8. The Root of the Tao

concept. We sense it in our bodies, – and use acupuncture to adjust ourselves to it – and we see it in the spontaneous happenings around us – and use the *I Ching* to correct our attitudes towards it.

The mathematical formulation of the field appears, in the *I Ching*, as hexagrams which describe the picture, message or meaning of events. According to Granet, the root of the Chinese word for 'Tao' looks like half a hexagram, consisting of three horizontal lines connected by a vertical line.[13]

The horizontal lines stand for heaven, man and earth, while the vertical line connecting the three is the Tao. This root word also stands for 'sage', 'priest' or 'king', according to Granet. Furthermore, Needham states that this root word is the basis of the terms for divination, calculation and playing.[14]

The crows' feet in the diagram on p. 44 were meant to symbolize human hands. Needham says that the diagram no doubt came from the game of chess. Chinese chess was related to astrology; the early astrologers rearranged the planetary constellations or fate, symbolized by the chess pieces on the board. Indeed, the representation of human hands in the diagram symbolizes that our interaction is an important part of fate.

The early Chinese sensed that human consciousness could enter the Tao and rearrange it as if it were a chessboard. Their idea was the

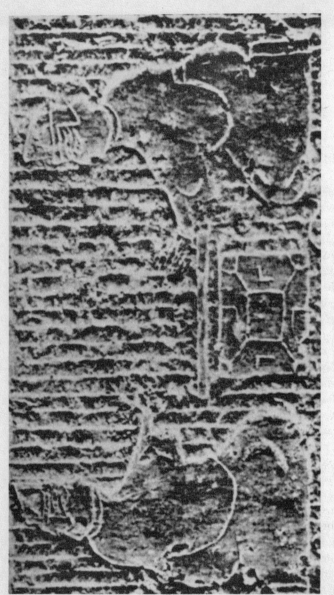

9. Divination, Calculation, Playing

prefiguration of the modern global facilitator, who intervenes, unfolds and interacts with the global field. The early Chinese sage or wise person was one who adjusted his life to the processes of the global mind. The mystical Chinese went further and implied that if you put yourself into Tao and became congruent with yourself, then the world, too, would fall into order. We are not just formed by the universal dream, but can interact with it as well!

The Global Mind and Individual Body

According to *The Yellow Emperor's Classic of Internal Medicine*, the Tao moves through all things, including the individual human body, which is structured by meridians carrying the polarities of the Tao.[15] If there is something wrong with the individual's attitude towards the universe, he becomes sick or suffers adverse fate, and his body manifests these difficulties as a block in the flow of Tao. The Chinese physician then applies acupuncture to the patient, adding or subtracting the necessary energy at the given meridian conduit, thereby bringing the individual back into Tao, into harmony with the world.

These divinatory theories and procedures connect our lives to a living global being, a gigantic anthropos whose mind we sense as a field. We feel the Tao with our bodies; we see it in all the spontaneous world events and synchronicities; we find it in our own dreams and experience it in our relationships. We are a small representation of what is happening around us. If something is wrong with us, it is because we either don't know or have trouble adapting ourselves to this universal mind.

And how do we know this global mind? We sense it as a god or spirit behind events. Earlier people projected this mind on to serpentine wisdom, fateful, benevolent or evil cosmic intelligence, maps from heaven or mathematical messages from the universe, cosmic signals requiring human reaction.

How can we find this global mind in our modern world? Ancient concepts of the dreambody appear today in our global projections, in the way we think of the world as a person suffering from chronic symptoms and problems, such as nuclear spills and acid rain, plagues like AIDS, and evil influences such as terrorists.[16] How we can interact with these fields will be discussed in later chapters. Regardless of how we look at it, the universe is a body, dreaming and requiring human consciousness as a psychological intervention.

Chapter Six

Global Suicide and Rebirth

Global myths inform us of many things, including our evolution, division, and conflicts, but they also speak of the combination of suicide and an optimistic rebirth. Some terrifying tales simply speak of the world's end. In this chapter I examine some of these mythical descriptions of our evolution.

The Doubling Birth

According to the Khandogya Upanishad, the entire universe, after being meditated upon, pops out of a cosmic egg.[1] In other cosmologies a god crafts the egg and then the egg splits itself into parts by doubling and quadrupling.

As in the last chapter, we see here that the world spirit creates itself through a meditative process, by sitting on the egg or by crafting itself according to its own mind. These developmental processes are similar to the propagation of new ideas. Ideas seem to pop up all by themselves in one or more persons, and then they propagate, spreading from the first creators to an avant-garde group which carries the ideas into the world, then to a section of the population which favours them, and finally to the wider majority.

The doubling, differentiating and enfolding, as seen in the above myths, are states which every group goes through. At first a group consists of an apparently unified network, then it differentiates itself, splitting into various groups with differing viewpoints and suffering from internal conflicts. If we think of a group or culture as a connecting idea, then the anthropos myths portray the tendency this idea has to differentiate itself.

Two Drives in Evolution

In some myths the doubling effect appears in the creator as an internal division in his personality. Take, for example, the Iroquois myth in which a great mother figure has twins in her uterus, opposites who battle against each other and who are both capable of creating the world. One, Firestone, cries out in the womb to the other, Maple Sprout,

> 'That is the place where we shall come out, it is the shorter way and the light is already shining through.' But the other said, 'Oh, no! We should kill our mother if we did that! We should go out by another way, the one which all human beings will take later. We will turn downwards.' [2]

But Firestone kills the mother by going quickly for the light, while Maple Sprout laments the murder. Maple Sprout symbolizes a traditional, primary Native American process, the tendency to integrate and get along with the environment, the great earth mother whence we all come. Maple Sprout wants to go the human way, the slow way, the way which honours history and respects the environment.

Firestone, on the other hand, represents a secondary process, that is, one with which the Native Americans do not identify. He is the one who rushes, who does not relate to the mother and cannot wait for things to happen organically. Firestone is that part of the Iroquois, and of humanity, which tends to destroy itself, by going for the light, by trying to discover the truth, by asserting itself at the expense of the whole earth. It is Firestone who creates both useful and destructive technologies.

A spokesperson for the Nez Perce tribe of the Wallowa Valley in Oregon describes how the Native Americans experience or project Firestone on to the white people.

> The White men were many and we could not hold our own with them. We were like deer. They were like grizzly bears. We had a small country. Their country was large. We were contented to let things remain as the Great Spirit made them. They were not, and would change the rivers if they did not suit them. [3]

Hearing this, I feel ashamed to be white, and yet at the same time, I know that Firestone is not only a white person's characteristic. The Firestone character can also be seen in the Third World's desire to buy Western technology and strive for American goals. The Third World is fascinated by Firestone; it needs him. He symbolizes its rush for technology, and he is simultaneously the part of our world which awakens us from unconsciousness.

Firestone kills the mother and ruins his community anthropos, yet his actions shock the earth into awareness. Many of us, and much of the Third World, have to change the river, take an active role in forcing change. Yet we also need to learn how to consider the whole community we live in and preserve her life while creating change. A global concept of community life needs to include both Maple Sprout and Firestone.

If Firestone is the rush for change, Maple Sprout is the awareness of pain and suffering that this rush brings. I have seen 'Maple Sprout' in the suffering of many people who sense that one hasty part of their community may inadvertently injure other parts and even the whole by concentrating only on its own struggle for being and its battle for change. Almost no one, it seems, thinks of others while speaking for himself.

In the Achomav Pima Native American myth of twin creators, Silver Fox and Coyote have a similar conflict to that of Firestone and Maple Sprout. One is the healing earth and the other kills it. Silver Fox creates the world out of his own body and is opposed by his great rival, Coyote, also called Elder Brother, who is always trying to undo Silver Fox's work. Silver Fox is also referred to as Earth Doctor and Earth Magician.[4]

Silver Fox, Earth Doctor or Earth Magician sound like those of us who want to 'heal the earth'. But who is Coyote, who makes the earth ill? Again, this hasty trickster has been projected, with obvious justification, upon the white people, as seen in the following speech from a Wintu woman. She was living in California in the 1950s near a gold mine where hydraulic blasting machines were being used.

When we burn grass for grasshoppers, we don't ruin things. We shake down acorns and pinenuts ... But the White people plough

up the ground, pull down the trees, kill everything ... They blast
rocks and scatter them on the ground ... How can the spirit of the
earth like the White man? ... Everywhere the White man has
touched it, it is sore.[5]

Here again, the Indian is the Earth Healer and the white person the
greedy and hasty Coyote. The images of the machines and of the
Coyote symbolize the aggressive, war-like drive of our nature, which
balances our drive to live quietly in peace, as in the past. One tendency
is sensitive and caring towards the earth, while the other is insensitive
and ruthless. These two complementary processes have many names:
revolt and homeostasis, adventure and security, haste and sensitivity.
We are living in a time when the old world is dying, in a time of
conflict between healing and killing.

Death and Rebirth of the World

German mythology is noted for its 'Götterdämmerung' in which the
cosmos kills itself. Most myths portray a global death followed by a
global rebirth. In the Persian Enuma Elish, for example, the world is
formed from the annihilation of the great anthropos woman, the
mother goddess Tiamat, who is slain by Marduk.[6] The tale of the great
Indian god, Purusha, is similar. Purusha, whose name means 'man', was
seen as the whole universe with a thousand heads and feet, extending
beyond the earth. According to legend, he is sacrificed and cut up.
Each part of him becomes a part of our known universe. His head is
the sky, his navel the air, his feet the earth; from his mind springs the
moon, from his eyes the sun, and from his breath comes the wind.[7]

Purusha and Tiamat symbolize a homeostatic cultural situation, the
status quo of an individual, couple, family, group or national system
which is not just destroyed, but must be sacrificed. What does this
mean for our everyday lives?

Individuals in the midst of radical transformation suffer the disorienta-
tion which accompanies the interruption of their old lives. Often they
feel like dying or killing themselves. Looking back, they can see how
necessary it was to let go of the old ways and try something new. The

old lifestyle often needed to go to pieces. Couples, too, experience this anthropos death, as their ideas about relationship change. Large group life is constantly disturbed by those who disagree and those who cannot conform. Nations live and die, ethnic groups disappear and are formed anew.

Though there is a force which wants to heal the earth, there is an equally strong and important one whose message is 'Kill the earth, we are dissatisfied and angry!' How many of you have, at one time or another, been dissatisfied with life and wanted to leave the earth? This desire represents the Firestone spirit that will no longer tolerate old conventions, and that overthrows old myths and rigid, sectarian religious views.

Picture 10 depicts this conflict in the Japanese New Year festival. The world, symbolized by a tree, is burned down in a battle between the older males on the platform and the younger ones on the ground.

But we must be careful about how change takes place, for burning down the world tree today is committing suicide. In the past we could afford to kill the trees, as there were enough of them around. But today we have to use our aggression more consciously. A new method of transformation, in which both destroying and creating have a place, needs to be developed. From now on, history must happen differently: it can no longer be an accidental occurrence, but must proceed through meticulous processing of internal and global tensions.

National History and Creation Myths

In Chinese mythology, Pan Ku is an anthropos figure that is the world and that simultaneously creates it. When he dies, the world as we now know it is created.[8] Likewise, in German mythology, the great and primeval giant, Ymir, a sort of field, (his name, 'Urgebraus', means the noise of the stormy sea) is killed by the more human Wotan and his two brothers. From the flesh of Ymir comes the earth, from his bones the mountains. Heaven comes from his skull, and the boisterous sea from his blood.[9]

Cultural myths, like the childhood dreams which organize our lives, pattern national histories. Thus, Pan Ku, the anthropos of Eastern civilization, is constantly dying, falling to pieces and being recreated. The truth of this can be seen in the constant turnover in Chinese politics, including the Cultural Revolution of the 1960s, and the 'Second Revolution' of the 1980s, Deng Xiaoping's sweeping reforms of China's economy, and his latest totalitarian regressions.

The death of Ymir can be seen in the bloody process of Germany throughout World War II. The violent and noisy Ymir was cut down, and from his emotionality arose modern Germany, literally split into parts.

Jewish tradition also has an Ymir figure, the original Adam, an immense anthropos that was spread over the entire world. In the mystical tradition, God kills Adam and reduces him to a small human being after his sin at the Tree of Knowledge of Good and Evil.[10] Before his death Adam contained 600,000 souls.

Afterwards, these were reduced in number. In cabbalistic thinking, the death and transformation of the world and of the Jews is not due to outer persecution, but to the relationship between Adam and God. It was God that reduced Adam and shattered his soul because of his transgressions, because Adam was unable to remove from his soul what God called the 'fallen sparks' which led him to transgressions.[11]

Applied to modern history, this Jewish myth implies that not realizing their own 'fallen sparks', their own Firestone, contributed to the Jewish people's suffering. Could it be that the creation of modern Israel is another chance to create a new Adam, one which will consciously use these fallen sparks of aggression and power instead of repressing or being possessed by them?

Developmental Anthropos Processes

When the anthropos dies in a family, large group or nation, the ruling idea dies. The blame is always projected on to an outer disturber, a group or enemy. A global view of evolution helps us to realize that threats to ourselves, our groups and the world are not only the work of the devil, but the potential demise of an old relationship paradigm. The destruction comes from within, from sparks which we have neglected, from revolution and restlessness asking for recognition.[12]

10. *World Death and Rebirth in Japan*

The first to die is the old identity of the group or nation, its ideology and beliefs. Peace dies, too, and we feel pain. Our pain is the pain of God killing himself, of Adam and Pan Ku going to pieces, of Ymir being sacrificed, or of the earth mother being murdered by Firestone.

The peace of the old world needs to be interrupted. Neglecting our own demonic sparks to keep order no longer works. The idea of racism, of keeping down those whom we feel do not belong, has run out of time, is becoming obsolete. The time for blind beliefs in outmoded ideologies has passed. The guiding ideologies of progress, socialism, democracy, Islam, Judaism, Christianity, Buddhism and even New Age thought twist, turn, transform and reawaken.

But how this transformation and awakening occurs, and the amount of pain it creates are not absolute laws of nature. From my global experience, which I will discuss in the last chapter, I now realize that the pain and joy of transformation depend upon our ability to process conflict.

Chapter Seven

Earth Magic and Science

Recent theories and events in physics, biology, and neurophysiology reflect old myths and support the experience of the world as a dreaming, transforming body which does not always respond to causal interventions. For example, Lovelock's 'Gaia Hypothesis', together with modern systems theory imply that the world is a living organism.[1] Many empirical telluric effects, such as the ability to divine the location of water, also fit under anthropomorphic systems theories.[2] Synchronicities in which dreams connect to outer situations are not causally explainable.[3] Some obvious and causal solutions do not seem to fit the problems, for example, increasing police protection at airports does not seem to discourage terrorism.

Science, in extending its causal roots, is attempting to create a new paradigm to explain the earth's acausal characteristics.

a. The Holomovement and the Tao

According to Bohm's holomovement theory, the world operates like a hologram, unfolding in a Taoistic manner.[4] Events in one part of the world are connected through the same pattern to events in other parts. As in the microcosm-macrocosm theory of medieval Europe, a part of the world carries the same pattern as the whole (see Chapter 5, Pictures 4 and 6).

Thus, synchronicity, which Jung defined as a meaningful connection between events, can also be understood as a holographic phenomenon in which events in one part of the world mirror those in other parts, since both parts have the same pattern for the observer at that moment. The Taoist would attribute the phenomenon to the dragon lines of the Tao, connecting the entire universe.

b. **Morphogenetics and God's Anima**

Rupert Sheldrake showed how, in the hundredth monkey effect, new behaviour learned by one monkey, and gradually learned by one hundred of his neighbouring monkeys, is suddenly observed in monkeys of other regions, where the first hundred monkeys could not have had any conceivable means of communicating the new behaviour to the monkeys of the other regions.

Sheldrake attributes this type of synchronicity to a kind of blueprint he calls a 'morphogenetic' field.[5] Patterns of events create behaviour and evolution in like beings. Events have a sort of 'blueprint'. The idea of a blueprint is similar to the medieval Christian concept of God's anima creating the world (see Picture 5).

Telepathic experiments which indicate that our brain does not necessarily contain what we call our mind support the morphogenetic field idea. Our mind can be spread over space at any given moment. Pribram, especially, has hinted that the mind is a hologram only partially located in the brain.[6] All of these theories imply the existence of a universal dreambody, a non-physical pattern, linked with events that have no known physical or causal roots.

c. **Non-locality and Micro-Macrocosm**

Other theories of modern physics sound similar. The breakdown of the principle of local causes indicates either that messages can travel faster than the speed of light or that the world sometimes behaves as if spatial distance had no meaning.[7]

This concept is understood in various ways. A magician would say that he can send messages and create effects which travel faster than the speed of light. A scientist would claim that there is no such thing as two separate localities. Jung would say that meaning organizes events. A storyteller from ancient times would explain that we are all part of the same gigantic anthropos. Yet all agree that our world is a field organized by patterns, not by time and space.

In ordinary terms, the parts of the world are connected through the psychology of the whole planet. There are no divisions between events in our inner world and the events of the outer world, as in the ancient micro-macrocosm idea.

d. **The Living Gaia**

The ancient views of the world which imagine the planet to be an anthropos are corroborated by Lovelock's 'Gaia Hypothesis', mentioned above, which implies that the world is a living organism.[8]

In the early 1960s, Lovelock, working with a team at the California Institute of Technology to investigate the possibility of life on Mars, came to the conclusion that the earth itself behaved as if it were a living organism, which he called 'Gaia', in honour of the ancient Greek earth mother.

Lovelock developed this hypothesis after noting the discrepancies between the real level of oxygen in the air (21 per cent) and the predicted level (0 per cent). Why has the actual composition of the atmosphere remained at an optimal level for the continuance of life, even though in a non-living (planetary) system oxygen should be rapidly absorbed and combined with other elements? Why has the amount of salt in the sea remained at its present 3.4 per cent over long periods of time despite the probability that it should rise? Why has a small quantity of ammonia remained in the atmosphere, neutralizing the air over unusually long periods of time and enabling the rain and soil to produce just the right amount of acidity to support life and give us food? And why has ozone remained in the upper atmosphere to shield us from ultraviolet radiation? Lovelock's answer to these enigmatic questions is that the planet is homeostatic.

Homeostasis

On the basis of these and other equilibrium characteristics, Lovelock concluded that the climate and the chemical properties of the earth have always been optimal to sustain life. Thus, the earth, oceans, land and air appear to be part of a gigantic system capable of homeostatically regulating life-supporting properties.

Just as our bodies and souls homeostatically maintain more or less the same personality, temperature and approximate volume for about eighty years, so the earth, too, has homeostatically maintained its properties despite internal changes and external events. Though Lovelock did not state that the earth was a living system, he implied that it behaved like a beehive which could support living systems.

Today, with the advent of systems theory, the entire biosphere can be seen as one living system, like an immense beehive with plants and animals, oceans and land, bacteria and whales, sky and forests as its various parts.[9] The concept of the earth as a living being is not just a myth but modern science.

Living Systems

According to systems theory, the world is an interconnected hierarchy of matter and energy. No part of a system can be understood on its own; each part is connected to every other part. James Miller, a pioneer in living systems theory, a particular branch of general systems theory, defines nineteen critical subsystems which characterize living systems.[10]

Peter Russel, one of Miller's students, lists and compares these subsystems with those in the human being, society and the earth, concluding that Gaia is, indeed, a living system.[11] I have adapted Russel's tables to the ideas of this work and have listed below some of the subsystems mentioned by Russel which illustrate the human nature of nations and the world. I have simplified his listing a bit in order to give the reader a more immediate overview.

The earth appears here as a living system, having its own brain, skin, muscles and hypothalamus. Not only the earth, but society, too, behaves like a living system. In other words, we can conceive of ourselves as parts of a human nation, which itself is a part of a larger personality, the globe. At all levels, we meet the same message over and over: we live inside a gigantic, dreaming being.

Subsystem	Level (Body)	Society (Nation)	Biosphere
Ingestor Brings matter and energy across boundary from outside	Blood	Transportation pipelines	Atmosphere allows light, volcanoes bring up minerals
Motor Moves system or parts of it	Muscles and bones	Cars, trains, tides	Climate changes, continental drift, wind
Internal Transducer Receives information about processes within system	Hypothalamus monitors salt and temperature	Public opinion polls, political parties	Animal and plant reaction to changing climate, floods, pollution, etc.
Memory	Entire brain	Libraries	Evolutionary adaptations seen in genes
Decider Receives information from subsystems and transmits back, controlling entire system	Brain centres	Governments	Soil, interspecies communication
Boundary	Skin	Customs, national borders	Earth's crust, upper atmosphere

Living Subsystems (Adapted from Russel)

Organization and Stratification of The Whole

Capra presents an excellent review of the new systems theory in his *Turning Point*.

The tendency of living systems to form multilevelled structures whose levels differ in their complexity is all-pervasive throughout nature and has to be seen as a basic principle of self-organization. At each level of complexity we encounter systems that are integrated, self-organizing wholes consisting of smaller parts and, at the same time, acting as parts of larger wholes. For example, the human organism contains organ systems composed of several organs, each organ being made up of tissues and each tissue made up of cells.[12]

Individuals, families, cities, nations and the world are represented in systems theory as the leaves, twigs, branches, limbs and trunk of a tree. Each unit of the living systems tree – the individual, family, city, nation, and world – is a self-organizing whole, and simultaneously part of a larger whole.

Humons

I propose to extend the meaning of the word 'human' by calling the units of the living systems tree 'humons'. A humon is self-organizing, thinks, feels and is human-like. Arthur Koestler calls these entities 'holons', stressing their connection with holograms.[13] If the whole is a hologram with human characteristics, then the individual, self-organizing units would be humons or little anthropoi in the image of the larger picture. Thus, humons are alive, have some degree of mind, and a tendency to perceive and be aware of their perceptions.[14] Just as each individual perceives, so families, groups, cities and nations also have particular perceptions and points of view, giving them individual characteristics. Capra continues this idea:

At each level the system under consideration may constitute an individual organism. A cell may be part of a tissue but may also be a micro-organism which is part of an ecosystem, and very often it is impossible to draw a clear-cut distinction between these descriptions. Every subsystem is a relatively autonomous organism while also being a component of a larger organism; it is a 'holon', in Arthur Koestler's term, manifesting both the independent properties of wholes and the dependent properties of parts. Thus the pervasiveness of order in the universe takes on a new meaning: order at one systems level is the consequence of a self-organization at a larger level.[15]

In other words, our behaviour and appearance are partly characteristic of the structure of the world we are living in. We can extrapolate and say that certain problems bother us because they are characteristic of the collective unconscious in which we live.

Bodywork shows us that disease in a given body part reflects the unconscious psychology of the entire personality. Likewise, it is important for the person's entire behaviour to integrate and reflect the behaviour of a troubled body organ.[16]

The Earth's Mind

From the systems' viewpoint, even concepts such as life and mind are aspects of the self-organizing patterns. Mind is defined as a tendency to organize activities in space and time. The systems theorists call this tendency to organize 'mentating', and claim that it is found in all living systems to one degree or another.[17]

The earth's mind – its capacity to organize and reorganize actions in time and space (to mentate) – provides a primitive means of creating identity. Groups also have a mind, in a sense, since they create an identity which differs from other groups. The acts of mentating, thinking and developing an identity create barriers to keep others out. *This* is us, and *this* is not-us. Keep out! Private Property! Knowing that our earth has a mind makes us more aware of groups' tendencies to rigidify their identities by making barriers and keeping out everything that doesn't belong.

Systems Theory and the 'Anima Mundi'

Gaia has a mind

which in turn must participate in some kind of universal or cosmic mind. In the words of Jantsch, 'God is not the creator, but the mind of the universe.' In this view the deity is, of course, neither male nor

female, nor manifest in any personal form, but represents nothing
less than the self-organizing dynamics of the entire cosmos.[18]

This systems idea reflects the medieval idea that God is the architect of
the world. The difference between today's thinking and past belief
systems, however, is that today's theories seem more abstract. Today
we theorize about the earth's fields, its mind, its holographic characteristics, its magic, nonlocal and super-relativistic behaviour. In the past,
people not only theorized about this god-anthropos-spirit, but also
dealt with it directly.

In fact, people knew that they had to be on good standing with the
global spirit in order to survive. For example, the Devadasi dancers of
India

> must dance at least twice daily before the chief idol of the temple
> . . . the only 'reason' why they should do so, I am persuaded, is to
> transfer their own bodily vigour, or the spiritual essence thereof, to
> the god-spirit which ensouls the idol in order that he should function
> with success on behalf of his worshippers.[19]

The 'primitive mind' is more advanced in that it senses its connection
with the telluric, anthropomorphic powers of the world. Earlier people
knew more about 'morphogenetics', and systems 'mentation'. We have
always experienced the spirit in the atmosphere which creates events.
Along with Einstein, Sheldrake, Bohm and others, we are now rediscovering that the world we live in has a background field with
many names and with many types of power.[20]

Whether we call it Jung's collective unconscious, telluric magic, the
living Gaia or the holomovement, the direction in which we must
proceed is clear: now that we have formulated the global dreambody,
we have to deal with it, help it, respect it, love it and interact with it.

Chapter Eight

Wake Up, Shiva

Perennial philosophy of India describes the universal dreambody as our unconscious perceptions, as an anthropos figure that uses our individual senses to know itself.

Arjuna, the archetypal warrior-apprentice of the *Bhagavad-gita*, near the end of his life, turns to his wise and divine tutor Krishna, to learn about the universe, Prakriti, or the field, and its own ability to observe, Brahman, or the knower of the field. Krishna explains that this body is called the field because a man sows seeds of action in it and reaps their fruits. He adds: wise men say that he who knows of the field is he who watches what takes place within this body.[1] According to this description, the anthropos is not just the body of an individual man, but the field of the world. This world is where we sow seeds and reap their fruits. Prakriti is the world we live in. That part of the anthropos which observes itself is called the Brahman. Krishna says: I am the knower of the field in every body.[2] Krishna then defines discrimination between the field and the knower as the highest kind of knowledge. Thus Krishna describes himself as cosmic awareness, which is found in everyone. He says that it is important to discriminate between the act of perceiving and the objects perceived, for otherwise we identify ourselves with what we see and lose our individual viewpoints and our capacity to differentiate ourselves.

Krishna speaks about three aspects of the personality. There is the ego, or in his words, 'man', which is capable of metacommunicating, or talking about, what is happening. Then there is an automatic perceiver, or Brahman, who uses our senses, and finally, there is the field, the things and objects we perceive. Simply said, the mind of the universal dreambody appears to us through our capacity to perceive, and the body of the universal dreambody appears to us through the things which we perceive. Brahman is the universal capacity in all people to see, hear, feel the body, move, relate to others and sense the world. Sensory awareness is an archetypal perceptual system characteristic of all human beings.

We, as individuals, have the ability and choice to become aware of our perceptions and of our awareness. For example, I see, but I am not always aware that I am looking. I hear, and when I am aware of what I hear, I can know the mind of the universal dreambody in myself. Yet I can also choose to ignore my awareness and think everything I sense is just me. That part of the universal dreambody which we channel becomes conscious when we become aware of our awareness, when we become aware of the fact that something in us is feeling, seeing, hearing, smelling, etc. Krishna tells us that the field, Brahman, is a human body with hands, eyes, feet, a face, a head, ears and movement.[3] Those aspects of our biosphere which do things would be his hands; those aspects which perceive are his eyes; the appearance of reality is his face; the meaningful connection between events is his head; and the motion and mechanism of the planet is his movement (see Picture 11). We saw above how early Christianity also imagined the world to be the body of God and, in the last chapter, how systems theory reflects Krishna's view that the supreme Brahman in this body is also known as the Witness.[4]

Movement can be voluntary, but in spontaneous movement it is not you that moves, but the universal dreambody that is moving, using you as a channel to dance (see Picture 12).

It is interesting to compare the Indian view with that of the Native American. Like Brahman, which manifests itself through the human senses, the Native American Winnabago 'Earth' also senses, sees, feels and knows.

> Holy Mother Earth, the trees and all nature, are
> witnesses of your thoughts and deeds.[5]

Here the witness is the earth's awareness. The earth itself is a channel that perceives. In India, the witness of the universal dreambody is the human process of perceiving and the body of the universal dreambody is the process of growth, healing and change. We find a similar idea about the earth in the words of Big Thunder of the Wabanakis Nation,

The Great Spirit is our Father, but the earth is our mother. She nourishes us; that which we put into the ground she returns to us, and healing plants she gives us likewise. If we are wounded, we go to our mother and seek to lay the wounded part against her, to be healed. Animals too, do thus, they lay their wounds to the earth.[6]

Disidentifying from Perception

In India, identifying perceptions as your own is the root of suffering.[7]

Bondage is the attitude which says, 'I am the doer and the enjoyer.' Who but Shiva can hear through the ears? Who but he can think with the mind and speak with the tongue?[8]

Suffering, according to Muktananda, is caused by identifying ourselves with the act of observation. Unconsciousness is believing that when you are sad, it is you who are sad, that when you are angry, it is you who are angry, and that when a slip of the tongue occurs, it is you who have been speaking.

To the Indian meditator, spontaneous acts and experiences are signs of the anthropos acting and experiencing itself. None of these things are personal unless we unconsciously identify with them or unless we take responsibility for them. Personal life begins with the development of a detached metacommunicator, with awareness of Shiva and Shakti, unconscious perceptions and observation. According to Muktananda's biographer,

These are extraordinary assertions. The 'I' who uses the senses and the organs of the body is none other than the supreme Lord who has limited Himself for his own sport or amusement. The only thing that prevents Shiva in the form of the individual from recognizing His own true identity is His false identification with His actions, His sense pleasure, and His thought. When we eat, Shiva is eating, when we hear, Shiva is hearing. To remain aware of this is the form of worship and meditation that Baba urges upon us.[9]

Consciousness here is a form of worship and meditation. Shankarananda leads us to an unusual thought: the supreme God is unconscious of

11. *Vishnu-Krishna Manifesting Divine Form*

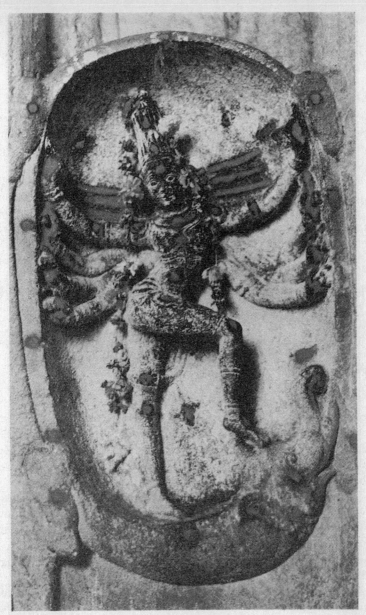

12. *Shiva's Dance*

Himself and needs our help. But is this unconsciousness due to divine 'sport'? Each should form her or his own opinion about this.

I think of the thousands of people that I have worked with individually and in groups. Most only rarely use their ability to become aware of the stimulus–response pattern of perception. We do not meditate upon our sensory system unless we have to, and we are thus only vaguely aware that our senses operate as archaic, spontaneous perceivers.

Hence, the ability to experience the universal dreambody as our perceptual system will have to wait for the moment when lack of awareness no longer works.[10] Perhaps the planet is now at the point of Shiva's awakening, at the point where we perceive and become aware of what we are perceiving.

Until now, the anthropos figures of this and earlier chapters symbolized our own growing awareness of awareness. The message from India, however, is stronger and says that *only when we perceive that we are perceiving will the anthropos awaken*. In this moment our unconscious god awakens.

World Politics

According to the *Bhagavad-gita*, all creation comes forth from the seeming union of Field and Knower, Prakriti with Brahman. Those who see the Lord within every creature, deathlessly dwelling amidst the mortal, see truly. Those who are aware of the Omnipresent hide the face of god beneath the ego no longer and therefore reach the highest bliss.[11]

If a friend gets angry with you and hurts your feelings, who hurt you? Who is responsible for making your friend angry? You cannot make yourself angry, it happens to you. The *Bhagavad-gita* explains that these happenings were caused by the universal dreambody. Consider the idea that when you fight with someone, it is Shiva fighting Shakti. You are not fighting, the anthropos is fighting with itself, it has an internal conflict with itself. Thinking that your actions are yours is a form of inflation.

Furthermore, the *Bhagavad-gita* states that if you think in this way, you should no longer be outraged at your opponent. Or rather, you would notice that your rage is the rage of the anthropos trying to work out a problem with itself. Your problem is the anthropos', so to speak, and you are its channel. The problems which hurt you and make you angry belong not only to you, but also to the whole world.

We are employed or dreamed up by groups to express conflicts. If we think in this way, we can then approach conflict-resolution processes from a very special perspective, with the neutrality of what I refer to as the spiritual warrior. When we are in a state of conflict, we are best prepared if we think that we are not just working for ourselves, but processing problems for the anthropos, the real earth. In this moment, inner work, spiritual training and global work are the same.

Part III

Global Process Work

Chapter Nine

Fluctuation, Disturbance and Change

Myths give us an immense overview, portraying the catastrophes and joys of life as internal conflicts of the awakening global organism. But these tales do not tell us how to facilitate global processes in order to minimize human suffering. Learning to facilitate global processes is therefore the next step and the third part of this book.

My experience with large groups and with thousands of people from all over the world in all sorts of emotional states indicates to me that our ability to facilitate global processes peacefully depends upon:

1. the overview of one person in a hundred who (a) realizes that every role in a field is important, (b) realizes that every living person is needed to fill these roles and (c) can help people to realize their potential in doing this
2. the willingness of at least five people in the same hundred, who are interested in these ideas, to work on themselves in different situations: alone, in relationships and in large groups.

The next chapters will define more precisely what is meant by 'overview', 'roles' and 'field' and what it means to work on oneself, in relationships and in groups.

Homeostasis

To my surprise, the difficulties in group transformation are not only due to the tenaciousness with which people hold on to the status quo, but also to the way in which the majority approaches minority issues and group disturbers. This corresponds to the systems view of change, as summarized by Capra:

> The basic dynamics of evolution, according to the new systems view, begins with the system in homeostasis — a state of dynamic balance characterized by multiple, interdependent fluctuations.[1]

The hidden factor in the homeostatic behaviour of real human groups is fear of change and pain. Our homeostatic behaviour and peaceful exterior stem from our fear of change and of the incomprehensible aggressiveness of the disturbers. Therefore, when we can, we neglect change.

Most individuals and groups produce or try to produce an apparently peaceful persona, a calm and collected mask for the world in order not to show conflict or internal tension. A more realistic picture would depict a system which aims to appear peaceful but is, in fact, perturbed by internal stresses, anger and fear. Groups, leaders and facilitators need to demonstrate more realistic behaviour by allowing some of their internal doubts and tensions to show.

Systems theory is a fairy-tale analogy of the world. Life begins with a homeostatic group, a kingdom at peace, able to maintain its identity over long periods of time. Each member, each role in the kingdom varies slightly, fluctuating in tiny ways while growing interdependently of others. The processes of one member or role are linked to those of another, so that the whole looks something like a woven fabric with its own particular design.

This tale does not stress the role of fluctuations in the dynamics of change but sees them as disturbances of the ideal, static state. Future systems theory will have to begin with change, and stasis will appear as one particular, momentary state.[2] In the future tale, the kingdom will be changing and flourishing: beggars and thieves, foreign witches and wise people will constantly excite the town, transforming and enriching it.

Present systems theory, however, is essentially oriented towards static states, not processes, and is therefore able to tell us only about that part of evolution which happens slowly. Thus we are at a bit of a theoretical disadvantage if we try to understand systems in the midst of rapid identity changes.

Repressing the Disturbers

> When the system is disturbed it has the tendency to maintain its stability by means of negative feedback mechanisms, which tend to reduce the deviation from the balanced state.[3]

We try to forget our bad dreams and not worry about little body problems. We seek to quiet loud children, soothe teenage frustrations and silence the neighbour's car. We medicate psychosis, take aspirin for headaches, forget the conflicts we read about in newspapers and try to maintain our individual, family, group and national identity.

We give negative feedback to change so automatically, unconsciously and rapidly that we think maintaining stability is a natural law. Though systems theory states that most systems react negatively towards change, and though most groups suppress the disturber, this tendency is not a natural law! We should say that, at the end of the twentieth century, the main reason the management of groups of people represses disturbers is because they do not yet know how to integrate the disturber's potential for lengthening the life of the system into the status quo.

There is, of course, also value in repression. Repression challenges the disturber to grow, to learn how to bring in new ideas in a more acceptable way. Repression enables the group to continue its task, at least momentarily. An individual with a body problem can neglect it and continue his day. A group can ignore a disturber, and the world can momentarily neglect the needs of the troubled Third World.

A Sick World?

The individual who represses little symptoms, however, must soon deal with syndromes or a major illness. Can we say that a group which always denies the disturbers becomes, by analogy, a sick group? Likewise, a world which always says 'good is what the powerful or the majority wants and bad is everything else which happens', will eventually become a sick world.

Though 75 per cent of the global population is in the Third World, it is the weakest financially. The Third World threatens the financial stability of the planet. Instead of listening carefully to their emotional and sometimes angry messages, we try to pacify them with materialistic solutions. We try to solve their outer problems by making them happy and quiet instead of processing the repressed hatred they feel towards the minority white population that has colonized them.

Racism, a World Disease

Let's work backwards. If the whole world were to take the Third World seriously, we would notice that what disturbs them is not only technological deficiency, but the fact that they have been colonized for so long; they suffer from lack of self-worth. Though colonization, in the strict sense of the word, has stopped, many Americans and Europeans still feel that anyone who does not look like, behave like, or believe as they do is not as good. White is the best, other skin colours are less good. This is racism. Behind the past and present world situation is an unconscious homeostasis which masks a global disease – racism in all its possible varieties, including any group's prejudiced views towards another group, whether a minority or a majority.

This global situation reflects our psychic life. Racism appears in many forms, whenever we forbid dreams, feelings and instincts to influence our behaviour. In relationships, we always think the other is wrong. And in public, we devalue and mistrust strangers, Everyone is a stranger, an outsider at one time or another, and thus everyone knows what it is like to be the underdog.

Positive Feedback to Fluctuations

Systems theory also speaks of more successful disturbances.

> However, this is not the only possibility. Deviations may also be reinforced internally through positive feedback, either in response to environmental changes or spontaneously without any external influence.[4]

A disturber gets positive feedback or reinforcement when the group discovers that it actually needs the disturbance. If we cannot successfully repress our symptoms, we are forced to live with them. One option is to accept disturbances or, in modern information lingo, to give them 'positive feedback'.

In process work, we go even one step further. We amplify disturbances, by increasing our awareness of them. We listen, feel, hear and relate more closely to them so that they tell us new things. When we are strong enough, we can listen to inner dream figures or body experiences and learn about possible new forms of behaviour. In developing global process work we must not only support the homeostasis but also focus on disturbances, for they are almost always the secret to change and to increased group longevity.

When we have trouble in relationships we focus on the disturbing information float. The essence of the disturbing unconscious field in relationships can always be found in body postures, facial motions and vocal tones of which we are unaware. I discuss elsewhere some of the many possible ways of transforming these disturbances into useful signals for change.[5]

In a non-equilibrium world, we cannot wait till trouble knocks on the door. We must begin to work with disturbances and fluctuations as part of everyday life. A group could do the same by aiding its disturbers, realizing that their behaviour and ideas are thoughts which everyone occasionally has. Of course, a highly intelligent disturber need not wait for a group to open up but can get positive feedback by first speaking in the terminology, language and belief system of the group before bringing in new ideas.

Process Language

If we define the primary process of a group or humon as the way that it identifies itself, then the secondary process will refer to disturbing ideas. Thus, in process language, change happens either when the primary process opens up to the secondary one, or when the secondary one learns to reformulate itself in terms of the primary one, without challenging it in an unnecessary way. In ordinary terms, we should notice people who are different from the average. Process work with the world means that each of us must approach the disturbers and their world view, incorporating their differences by valuing them. Why ask the minority to care for themselves? They represent needs which everyone has repressed or forgotten. If you wait too long, you or your group becomes overly selective and segregative, and the majority feels ill because it loses the renovative message of the minority.

If you are one of the disturbers, one of the few who are different, do not believe naïvely that you will be accepted by the world. The beginning of global awareness for you means introducing yourself in their language, valuing not only your behaviour, but theirs as well. Don't expect only the majority to have the awareness you are asking for; have awareness yourself, and experiment by taking your side and their side as well.

Powerful Deviations from the Norm

The stability of a living system is continually tested by its fluctuations, and at certain moments one or several of them may become so strong that they drive the system over an instability into an entirely new structure, which will again be fluctuating and relatively stable.[6]

In a large business organization I recently worked with, the least powerful group, the secretaries, complained of feeling abused by the sales personnel and the boss. They forced the issue until the boss, against his earlier desire, decided to allow my staff to help resolve the problem. A small conflict resulted in minor changes in the system's structure, the boss and the sales personnel. Everyone seemed happy and the organization once again settled down, but with a new structure.

A year later, I indirectly learned from this group that I had not been useful. We discovered from talking with the administration that our goals had been different from theirs: we were accused of not wanting to follow their process but ours! We had hoped that the organization would be interested in our paradigm of continuous change. Their goal was to work together better; thus, we found ourselves in an unexpressed conflict with the administration, a conflict that we were not sufficiently conscious of to address even at the time.

Thus, the bosses viewed us as having been helpful, but troublesome, because they thought we sided with the disturbing secretaries. We had to admit that although we had aimed to be conflict-resolution experts, in fact we had created conflict, because we were unconscious of our own viewpoint! We did not intentionally side with the secretaries but seemed to do so since we were so interested in change. A global attitude towards the organization would have been to accept its many goals, and not expect unconsciously that everyone should have ours. I shall show later how supporting and taking sides with the underdog is a way in which the UN also creates conflicts.

Edges

There are various edges or barriers which groups create to keep out the unknown.

1. *Fearing the unknown*, or Xenophobia. This makes us create rigid hierarchies and barriers to protect us against new things. Our xenophobic behaviour makes us look angry and unwilling to change.

2. *Avoiding emotional issues* at all costs. For example, someone in a large group mentions a forbidden topic or attacks someone else for being rigid. Everyone fears these emotional issues and neglects them. Later we go back to these, point out the barrier or edge and reaccess the various viewpoints and feelings this brings up. If we don't go back to those issues, they cycle, and come back again at another time.

A conflict-resolution study group mentioned that some of the outsiders were not feeling at home in the group. The group neglected this issue because it seemed disturbing and unnecessary. Later we went back to this point and discovered that everyone felt left out or, at least, 'out of it', because nothing emotional or real was happening.

Facilitators need courage to stay near these difficult points or edges, because without the ensuing processes the group misses the spirit and energy that could bond them together. The community spirit appears most distinctly (if paradoxically) at the edge in the form of individual emotions and interests.

3. *Avoiding our own opinions*. Another group edge appears in discussing *third parties*, that is, other people or groups that are not present.

Nations do this all the time, by slandering other nations and creating symmetrical projections. We have to learn to pick up projections and incorporate the third parties into the present by saying that what the 'others' think we think too, but we are just shy to admit it. The people we slander, gossip about or accuse can always be found in the present.

4. *Avoiding the present.* Still another edge is referring to events as if they happened only in the *past*, or will happen only in the *future*. For example, instead of only thinking about the possibilities of a new world, our life would be richer now if we lived the future we are talking about.

5. *Fearing chaos* is another edge. The majority fears chaos, as well as fearing the disturbers. The disturbers fear speaking up and losing their position in the group.

The disturber afraid of losing her job, money, or social standing can discover that she is actually being used by the group to be a disturber. If she realizes that she is a channel for a possible new group idea, she will be able to present her feelings in a way which will endear her to everyone. More detailed discussion about such group work will be shown in the next chapter.

The value of edges is to warn us about dangers, to keep us away from issues for which we are unprepared. The disadvantage is that by keeping us away from certain topics, we never learn how to deal with them and must wait until they overcome us. Moreover, most of the edges we have in groups are projections of rigidity which we ourselves help to create.

The best way for leaders to deal with their edges and fear of chaos is to learn how to work through strong emotions and tensions rapidly to minimize pain.

Non-equilibrium Development

> The classical theory [of evolution] sees evolution as moving towards an equilibrium state, with organisms adapting themselves ever more perfectly to their environment. According to the systems view, evolution operates far from equilibrium and unfolds through an interplay of adaptation and creation.[7]

Though much change occurs far from equilibrium, we have until now focused only on near-equilibrium conditions. Thus, we never seem prepared for rapid change, which may be why our global process methods, our rituals and world peace organizations have not been as helpful as we had hoped in tense situations. Our work must be augmented with non-equilibrium methods which give us security in the midst of rapid change. This will be the work of Chapters 10 and 11.

Individuals and Field

Moreover, the systems theory takes into account that the environment is, itself, a living system capable of adaptation and evolution. Thus the focus shifts from the evolution of an organism to the coevolution of organism plus environment.[8]

There is no such thing as independent change. The world changes, and calls us or dreams us up to fill one of its roles, and changes us. Or we change and touch everything in the environment. In global process work, the switch in focus from individual change to field change occurs continually and fluidly. For example, when a group has tried its best to work on a problem, the momentous change of one individual will change everything. I think of a group conflict where the ten black members of a 140-person community felt that the whites did not pay attention to them. A few white people stood up and said they mistrusted the blacks, whereupon the blacks responded with denigrating statements. An impasse was reached, and the whole group froze.

Then, one white man decided to risk his worst fears, and turned his back on one of the black men. For a moment the whole room was filled with terror. The black man then reached out, put his arms around the front of his 'opponent' and embraced him. The white man broke down and cried and everyone embraced with true feeling. The group edge was crossed by one or two men who changed everything. But without the earlier group work, they could not have done their work. Individual, couple and group changes happen interdependently.

Chapter Ten

Group Process Structure

Question: What are you doing when you are not reflecting on yourself?

Answer: You are automatically following the programme of your doings, your primary process.

Question: What does a group do when it is not reflecting on itself?

Answer: It is trying to perpetuate its identity by attempting to accomplish its goals.

Self-reflection occurs in many ways; the most thorough or deepest probably occurs when conflicts between parts of the individual or group cause self-doubt. Complete reflection involves, at some point, knowing what you intend to do and also knowing what you are doing which you did not intend.

Interventions in Process Work

Interventions in individual and group work are methods for enhancing self-reflection. The most successful interventions are always those which appreciate and use the conscious and unconscious methods an individual or group is already employing in the moment.

The **process-work philosophy** behind interventions is that those things we are consciously and unconsciously doing will aid us in solving problems and enriching our own experiences.

I shall call any method or idea which enables us as individuals or groups to make our behaviour more accessible and useful 'process work'.[1] The basic idea behind process work is the belief that there is an inherent intelligence in human beings which appears when all parts of their behaviour are made equally accessible. Global process work is a wide-spectrum attempt to apprehend events at all levels. Such work values homeostasis and equilibrium as well as change.

Thus a **global process-work** attitude applied towards an individual, such as a woman with a backache who asks for medication, would be to prescribe a solution for her problems. If this does not work, and she is interested in other methods of treatment, we would make the experience in her back accessible to her through dream or bodywork so that she could live the experience in her back in her everyday life, in her relationships and in her worldly activities. The channel or mode in which we work at a given moment depends upon the modalities which she is consciously and unconsciously using at that moment.

Ideally, process work focuses on the **indivisible unit** and the channels which are used in a given moment. At any time, this unit might break up into smaller, indivisible units or unite with others to form a larger one. Thus, to work with a large group, we will have to be able to deal with individuals, couples and the interactions between the people. We should also be able to work with subgroups, with the large group as a whole, and with its relationships to other groups.

Philosophy and Interventions

It is virtually impossible to separate belief from method. Thus, the belief that everything necessary for a solution can be found now in the person asking for help is already an intervention.

We are Doing what we Need

This is an open-hearted, supportive idea which solves many problems by itself. Our beliefs about ourselves and others are interventions in that they guide our decisions and make experiences available or, in some cases, unavailable to us. Practically everyone responds well to the belief that what they need is already present. We must obviously unconsciously believe this, otherwise we would not stick so stubbornly to our impossible behaviour! Thus, process-work paradigms are interventions in the sense that they value and make conscious what people are either consciously or unconsciously doing.

It is important to be aware of the paradigm we are using as facilitators in order to be able to give up our methods if they do not work. The best process work attempts to follow the total situation, and does not request that everyone be conscious at all times, unless this is the real nature of the group at that moment. Some of our beliefs are less useful than others in helping people. For example, if we believe that everyone should be selfless, we will have trouble being useful because interventions based upon this belief are inconsistent with people's actual behaviour.

Those of us interested in psychology must be careful about our own beliefs about consciousness: *consciousness is sometimes necessary for some people in some groups, but not for everyone, all the time, in every group.*

To be able to follow the apparently endless proliferation of possible human processes, we must rely upon our feelings, past experiences and intuitions. However, since there are always new situations which do not fit our expectations, it will be very helpful to be able to appreciate two of the most common group structures: hierarchies and networks.

Hierarchical Group Structures

Hierarchical structures have identified leaders and are easy to recognize since they are so common. Even our inner lives are organized hierarchically. Our conscious beliefs act as the leaders, and the rest of our parts try to adapt to these beliefs, though frequently in vain. Hierarchical thinking has the advantage (when all parts and people are in agreement with it) of getting things done most efficiently. The disadvantage of hierarchical thinking is that it usually undervalues the leadership potential of the 'followers'.

Networks

The study of social movements of the 1960s and 1970s led to the discovery that leaderless groups also have definite structures.[2] These group structures, called networks, are present in all groups, even in apparent hierarchies; thus, we shall be focusing upon network structures.

Networking is a 'soft' term for scientific systems theory, according to Lipnack and Stamps.[3] A characteristic of a network is that the boundaries are frequently difficult to define. For example, determining who belongs in the network is a most difficult question to answer. A human network is characterized by feelings and beliefs, and by clusters of interactions around these beliefs rather than by fixed boundaries which include and exclude people. Those who 'belong', according to Lipnack and Stamps, are like cells which support given organs at one moment and move on to another organ in the next.

Let us say that a network is a field which radiates from an idea or an ideology, rather than from a fixed number of people doing things together. The field of network appears in groups but is larger than the group. We shall see in the next chapters how these definitions themselves become interventions.

SPIN

To work with fields it is important to know more about their structures. I am infinitely grateful to Virginia Hine's important research in this area. Her structural discoveries may be summed up in the acronym SPIN.[4] According to Hine,

S stands for Segmented, 'composed of autonomous segments which are organizationally self-sufficient'. They are decentralized segments, connected by overlapping membership and mobile leadership.
P stands for Polycephalous, or having many heads.
I means Ideology. Networks agree on certain values and ideologies.
N means Network, or specific communication forms.

The 'soft' definition for a network given by Lipnack and Stamps is

a portion of the world that is perceived as a whole and is able to maintain an identity in spite of the changing identities in it ... A network is made up of parts that themselves have identities ... A network is a whole of interacting parts with whole identities.[5]

SPINAG

In other words, a network is a primitive, mentating organism. I would like to add two more characteristics to Hine's network: A and G, extending SPIN to SPINAG. A, awareness, and G, garbage, or repressed material, are essential characteristics of every human group and we will need these characteristics to apply process work to strongly non-equilibrium network situations. Understanding processes of radical change requires valuing the awareness and repressed material of networks, groups or humons. Let us look more closely at the structure of SPINAG.

S and P: Segmented and Polycephalous

Groups of people segment themselves, creating and assigning the leadership roles for various reasons. Members of networks migrate to different places, have power battles, divide leadership, and find different ways to do the same thing. The Swiss psychologist, Jurg Willi, states that ideas differentiate themselves.[6] Thus, it might be that segmentation and differentiation occur because any given belief has many different sides to it.

Segmentation also occurs because, independent of ideology, there are natural differences among people. Groups consist of more experienced and less experienced members, women and men, teachers and learners. Members can also be differentiated by their geographical areas, and each region's economic and political issues.

The whole planet, too, has different sides. From earliest times, the world segmented itself into forces from the west and east, north and south. This global segmentation still holds today. Economic groups at the UN categorize themselves in terms of North (most of Europe, the US and Russia) versus the South (the Third World). Segmentation is not simply geographical but can also be symbolic. For example, Spain and Portugal, really part of Europe, are assumed by UNCTAD to belong to the South, since economically they belong to the poorer. Third World.[7]

In brief, we can say that segmentation occurs in individuals and groups as a sign of diversity, completeness or wholeness. The more sides we have, the more differentiated we are.

Roles, Occupation and Friendships

Groups separate, segment, and bring people together. The factions or roles in a group call on people to fill them. Thus, if a certain faction or role is not sufficiently filled in a group, those who are closest to its characteristics will be drawn together to fill it. Network processes use people to fill a role, and thus, we may temporarily find ourselves befriending people, not because we like them, but because they 'populate' the same role as we do in a group or global scene.

Sociological theory calls role occupation 'person selection' and implies that if someone is not there to fill a role, society will create such a person. '. . . Fierce warriors appear because there are battles to be fought.'[8] In empirical-relationship work, we have seen how the behaviour of an individual can be influenced or 'dreamed up' by a field.[9]

For example, two Protestants in a Catholic Swiss mountain village who do not like each other under normal circumstances suddenly become friends when, at a village meeting, they are pressed together by community circumstances to defend the Protestant position at a town meeting.

Roles usually have longer lives than people. Gandhi was killed, but his role survived: the drive to settle world problems through meditation and introspection. We can legally forbid the idea of segregation so that blacks are dealt with more fairly, but racism still persists. Though blacks now have a better position in the US, the Third World has become the world's second-class citizen. Our trade agreements with the South concerning·technological transfer of ideas and machinery are more segregational and restrictive than we would ever allow in our own country.[10]

We cannot get rid of the roles or parts of a group, whether we forbid them or kill the people in the roles, for a group is a humon, a belief system or idea. We must differentiate people from the roles they fill, and find out what beliefs and ideologies the roles themselves represent.

People and roles are different. An individual has many parts, and can assume all the possible roles in a group. A group role is usually more one-sided. For example, a family with a mother, father and child has three roles. But the woman does not always have to play the mother role any more than the man must play the father role. Cultural and biological processes tend to create roles, but the freedom to be an individual enables any one of us to fill any role we need to. Thus, at a given moment, the man, woman or child could be the baby, father or mother.

Real and Apparent Leadership

If we understand the leader as just another role, we see that the power projected upon our leaders is apparent, not absolute, since real leadership comes from those who are aware of the process trying to happen in their community. The apparent leaders are representations of field roles, which are parts each of us can and must sometimes fill. Each one of us occasionally has the energy, knowledge and excitement to contribute to this role. I think that one of the decisive, imminent changes in global consciousness is to realize that the apparent 'leader' is a form, a role, or a symbol for insight and power that each of us sometimes identifies with and is responsible for contributing to our communities.

The apparent leader of a country symbolizes its primary process, and the leader's shadow, his or her secondary process, similarly reflects that of the nation. For example, the president may have a strong religious commitment, but may also be dishonest, egotistical or abusive in private. These are secondary characteristics, which are allowed only to the smallest degree. If they become too strong, he won't fit the primary role any more.

On the other hand, if a leader represents only the primary process of the country, or just the opposite, namely the secondary one, he will not be able to stay in office long. The global field will not support one-sided leaders except, perhaps, in times of war when all the roles in the field are one-sided. Thus, a rational person without any spiritual feeling will be as unacceptable in the leadership role as a spiritual person without a reality function. What is essential about the leadership position is the spirit of the role, and not necessarily the entire complexity of the person filling it. Whoever comes near this role is dreamed up by the field to be a public servant of the magnetic powers of the community. If her personal psychology changes and she no longer fits the primary role we dream up, or if she stands too much or too quickly for a secondary process of the community, she will be forced to leave office, or be killed, become ill or be forgotten by the voters. A little psychological knowledge about global fields could be helpful to world leaders! The leader's power is only a reflection of the majority's identity, which is created by our concept of community. No one listens to the leader; they listen to the field role and filter out the personal information about the real leader that does not quite fit the role. We unconsciously focus on the president without recognizing the field which created the role, and thus we falsely identify the person with the role. And when she doesn't fill it properly we complain, instead of realizing that we are needed to fill it too.

The Influence of the Individual

Do we as individuals have any importance or influence in the larger global field? If you follow your own life's process, you automatically play the role you must. Even if your role is to be the silent one who feels but cannot speak, you are essential to the field. You may play an unpopular or even a publicly unrecognized role but you are still playing a 'leading' role in the sense that only when all roles are consciously represented, can the field operate humanely and wisely. Each role is a leading one because the field we live in is created by the tension and interaction between all its roles.

Filling the role of the leader, the follower, the silent one, the wise one or the disturber is essential for the life of the community. Only when all the roles are filled and interact, can the entire field discover its own human and self-governing capacity.

Now leadership is beginning to take on a new and extended meaning. A leader is anyone at any moment who represents one of the roles in a field. Being yourself is a political activity today, as it has always been! We are only just now realizing that our awareness can be as creative as a bomb is destructive. Just being aware can have immediate but also distant effects on others because of non-local field principles. In a world of nonlocality, every thought and feeling is global.

Becoming identified with any one role is important for us and our communities but it is also one-sided. Each of us has all the roles within, we are just too complex to be identified with only one for long. Roles belong to the community; we need to fill them, and step out, take on other roles, and finally just be ourselves.

I: Ideology

Virginia Hine's seminal message is,

> The S, the P and the N represent organization factors which can be handled at the sociological level of analysis . . . but the power of the unifying idea adds a qualitatively different element to the equation. The power of a unifying idea . . . lies in a deep commitment to a very few basic tenets shared by all.[11]

According to Hine,

> One of the crucial tasks of the immediate future is to clarify and expose the underlying assumptions that provide the ideological glue for the [networks] emerging at the various levels of the global structure. The key to the future may very well be conceptual rather than organizational.[12]

Let's investigate this 'ideological glue'. The value system or ideology which binds a group together may be understood as a story or myth. In studying global beliefs, Michael and Anderson indicate that the main (or primary) world ideology until now has been the belief in progress, which

> . . . once served as a unifying framework within which people of vastly different political persuasions could agree to disagree . . . [It] no longer commands the same respect. Opinion polls report widespread erosion of confidence in the future. There is a strong strain of primitivism in the West today, a forceful rejection of the myth of progress . . .[13]

Michael and Anderson identify six world ideologies today, the last two being 'post-modern' ideologies:

1. **Progress** is the idea that everyone should strive towards the Western ideal of growth, development, and an industrialized democracy.

2. **Fundamentalism** is based on the notion of absolute inerrancy of the Scriptures, and preaches the return to a society governed by traditional religious values; it rejects change and modern scientific thought, and defends national sovereignty.

3. **Islam** emphasizes an uncompromising and rigorous monotheism and strict obedience to a God and his law of the predetermination of good and evil.

4. **Marxism** is the idea that all history is a struggle between an exploiting and an exploited class, and that class struggle will ultimately culminate in a classless society with rights for all.

5. The **Green** ideology is an ecological and economic idea championing environmental awareness, pacifism and the preservation of endangered species, as well as political freedom and rights for oppressed groups.

6. The **New Paradigm** ideology believes in sudden leaps to a new way of being and understanding. It is connected with the Green group but also embraces big business, high tech and the future exploration of space.

Though there are many more world ideologies, I will content myself here with these. For the moment, I want to stress that a given ideology creates a morphic field around a network or group; the ideology is a myth, a saga, a hope for humanity. Ideologies have unlimited power; they give us reasons for living. They are our most prized possessions, but also our most dangerous liabilities, for they operate with an hypnotic magnetism far from consciousness.

Ideologies are not only frameworks offering us meaning, but can also become rigid systems, perhaps even prisons, for all who do not obey. They inspire and inhibit, give us vision yet blind us to events which do not fit. We need only think of how American Fundamentalists refused to allow the teaching of evolution in the public schools. Similarly, those who believe in progress today refuse to accept facts which show that progress is related to environmental deterioration. Marxist theorists neglect the statistics of low productivity from

Marxist economies, and fundamentalists resist some findings of modern science.

Psychology, too, has ideologies and blind spots. The psychological network is held together by the belief that people can change with the help of other people. But the network is divided into many segments: the Freudians, Jungians, behaviourists, Gestalt therapists, body workers, process workers, Adlerians, family therapists, NLP practitioners, Buddhist meditators, and many modern medical practitioners. Each of these segments or subgroups is suspicious of the others and is often blind to their own and the other groups' ideologies.

Knowing the danger of the group's ideology, we must ask ourselves why we belong to groups. One answer is that we identify a group with the paradigm and we need the paradigm for individual growth. Another reason is that group ideologies and the resulting friendships promise support to us as individuals, although, in fact, a group supports us only as long as we believe in its ideology. When we change, the support we once received is gone because much of it was never personal.

Groups also give us hope. Even though the behaviour of individuals in a group may not reflect their ideology, we always hope that one day the group will change. We sense the psychic force behind an ideology and mistakenly project it on to a group or individual. Separating groups from individuals will now belong to our growing global awareness.

N: Network

Which forms of communication do networks use? Groups communicate by speaking together, writing letters, telephoning and using video and audiotapes. Most groups do not metacommunicate about their psychological behaviour except secondarily in the form of gossip. Gossip and even dreaming are secondary forms of communication since they are spontaneous, unintended message exchanges. We can dream about things we want to keep secret from others!

Thus all groups are segmented, polycephalous, ideological networks with various methods of communication.

A: Awareness

Groups vary according to their awareness. All groups possess some degree of self-awareness and some ability to reflect and work with themselves. Our awareness of how groups operate shows that those individuals who speak most represent only the identified primary process, and those who are not spoken to or who remain silent belong to the group unconscious, its secondary process, which is usually not identified with. The disturber, the identified patient, also belongs to the group's secondary process.

Group awareness means understanding that all roles and segments are necessary to create and differentiate a field, and that everyone is needed to fill these positions.

Awareness also means noticing when groups repress emotional issues and disturbers. Abandoning difficult issues, changing themes, speaking only of the past or future, or about absent members are edges, unconscious methods of avoiding essential aspects of the group spirit.

A heightened group awareness perceives frustration and tension, feels group atmosphere and identifies the various polarities and differences creating this tension. Having awareness means noticing the tendencies in groups to cast out unknown or new members and to create insider and outsider groups.

Being on the 'inside' usually refers to being closest to the identified leadership positions, to those who seem to have the power, to those who are the apparent representation of the group ideology or group spirit. Being 'in' is not merely a function of the time spent near the leadership. You can be 'in' simply by believing in an ideology. That is why you may believe in an ideology, but not the group, feel like an outsider, but dream that you are inside.

G: Garbage

The 'garbage pail' is a humorous way of identifying the most tense area of group life. Garbage is the shadow: the secret, evil, forbidden yet beautiful thoughts that we quickly discard. Good psychic economy means processing the garbage as frequently as needed.

Human groups are all characterized by the same garbage. Garbage becomes manifest in the secret thoughts we have about each other: Who earns what? Who is strongest? Who is weakest? Who is most intelligent or most beautiful? Who sleeps with whom? Who is an insider? Who is an outsider? Who has power? Who really determines what happens?

Though fascinating, garbage is discarded because it opposes group ideologies, which usually have little humour about their shadows. Networks, like people, do not like to focus on their shadows and prefer to throw them out, creating information floats and troubled atmospheres. When the garbage is processed it always creates greater connection and spirit between members. Yet most organizations are hopeless about ever bringing their garbage to light.

At a recent supervision seminar I was giving in Switzerland, some of the students were more advanced than others, and the less advanced ones felt left out and neglected. The outer facts were simply true. At that time, I was concentrating more on the advanced students.

We began to process the garbage, the feeling of being left out, and a beautiful experience ensued. Some participants played the insiders, others the outsiders, and having complained and fought for a while someone noticed how quiet it was in the room. Another person shyly said that she heard a melody and began to hum it. The song she heard was 'Dona', and the words were:

On a wagon bound for market, there's a calf with a mournful eye,
High above him there's a swallow, winging swiftly through the sky,

Chorus:
How the winds are laughing, they laugh with all their might,
Laugh and laugh the whole day through and half the summer's night,
Dona, dona, dona, dona, dona dona dona dona.

Stop complaining, said the farmer, who told you a calf to be?
Why don't you have wings to fly with, like the swallows so proud and
     free,

Chorus

Calves are easily bound and slaughtered, never knowing the reason why,

But whoever treasures freedom, like the swallow must learn to fly.

Chorus

As she hummed it, another man explained its meaning. He told us that this song was written by a Jew in a concentration camp during the Second World War, who, like the calf, was bound for the gas chambers. The song was smuggled out by a priest. The meaning of the song is that a calf does not know that there is a bird, a free-flying swallow above. The tortured outsider must remember the spirit of freedom and detachment of the bird that is 'so proud and free'. Being outside or inside is relative, a momentary role within a field. Knowing this brings true freedom, the soaring freedom of the free-flying swallow above.

After the song, no one spoke. The music melted the barriers separating inside from outside and transformed the tension into a sense of eternity.

Chapter Eleven

World Process Theatre

Recognizing a group's structure allows us to follow its processes, to make its experiences more useful and to arrive at unimaginable and unpredictable solutions. Some of the basic components and related interventions which we shall deal with in this chapter are summarized below. The interventions are divided into subcategories of SPINAG (see Chapter 10 for a full explanation of SPINAG).

Segmentation
> sensing
> blank accessing
> dreaming up
> amplifying

Polycephalous structure
> polarizing
> sorting out the different roles
> intervening
> encountering
> identifying different process modes

Ideology
> identifying and respecting the group ideology

Networking
> identifying and working with network methods

Awareness
> understanding primary and secondary processes
> becoming aware of signals, feedback and feelings
> working with altered states; recognizing the drive for wholeness; picking up group projections

Garbage
> dealing with repressed issues and information float

SPINAG

An exhaustive description of each intervention would be a book in itself. Rather, assuming that the reader understands that process-work training is experiential as well as intellectual, I will briefly try to outline different ways of working with fields and groups.

Segmentation:

Sensing

This is the perception of overtly and covertly expressed feelings and opinions. All of us sense the atmosphere, the global field, by the language people use, their tone of voice, their facial expressions and by their movements – restless, stiff or relaxed. In all situations, each one of us has vague feelings and tensions, a sense of anxiety, discomfort or fear. We sometimes detect things which are not happening overtly, and we sometimes overlook our own sensitivity. In a rough group, we overlook someone who might be hurt. Conversely, in a sensitive group we overlook the rough, unsentimental person. Thus, the first intervention is to sense feelings, to believe them and to ask about them. 'Who feels what?' or 'Who is feeling something in this corner of the room?' are questions which allow the atmosphere to express itself.

Blank Accessing

This is a sensing method which presents an empty 'blank' for a group to project into or express itself with. Open statements such as 'I feel something but do not know what it is', or 'Someone is thinking something here' can help people sense what is happening in groups.

Dreaming Up

Sensitive facilitators frequently experience group emotions which have not yet been expressed. The facilitator gets 'dreamed up' to pick up a group 'dream', that is, a community feeling, vision or opinion needing more support. There are always many secondary processes, or back-ground parts, issues and feelings which groups do not sufficiently represent because these parts may not be welcomed. Repressed or otherwise unknown experience searches for expression, and the wise facilitator, who senses this experience, will note it, work internally on how it affects her, and finally give it back to the group.

I remember once working with a large group which was in a tough, violent phase of its life. The compassionate, sensitive part was unrepresented and consequently, I found myself oversensitive and angry at them for their insensitivity! I worked on my own process here, and was then overjoyed to notice at the next meeting that a large part of this group felt as I did. As their sensitivity came out, I felt better and the whole community arrived at an incredible and intimate conclusion.

Most sensitive facilitators unconsciously take everything they feel to be their own. In global work, however, we have to suspect that some of our feelings are both inner and outer.

Amplifying

Once we sense a given atmosphere, the next step is to amplify this sensory experience. Group atmospheres usually do not express themselves directly, and hence they tend to amplify themselves as would a body symptom. A rule of thumb in dealing with all human situations is that unconscious states seek our attention. If we do not bring them out, they will do so themselves, and at that stage they usually overwhelm us.

For example, in any gathering, whether a religious group, a rock-concert audience or a military training group, fears of inadequacy, loneliness, expectations, or the need for the numinous are *feelings* floating in the field. Processing these feelings reduces the information float and heightens the members' participation in the group.

Polycephalous Structure:

Polarizing

The simplest way of processing feelings is to discuss, demonstrate and act out the feelings in the different roles. Each role communicates with another role. Which role is the inadequate person speaking to? Is it the tyrant who makes others feel inadequate? Each role in a field can be understood as a reaction to another role, and polarizing these two roles clarifies the field.

A gifted facilitator will notice if the roles have been properly identified in the group field by the enthusiasm or lack of energy with which participants join in. If many people do not feel like joining in, then another role in the field needs to be brought in. The feelings people have will show which roles have not been identified. Finding the roles in a global field is essential to understanding it. By taking over the vague information float, we are giving it a chance to channel and differentiate itself; we are helping it create instead of pollute us.

Certain people in a field function as the background leaders and rarely manifest themselves, in part because their roles are not allowed or recognized. The primary group process needs awakening here. For example, we need only think of the quiet 'person', perhaps a woman behind a powerful leader. Such women frequently play the role of spiritual guide for the group. But many people have unrecognized or even unwanted group roles, and do not feel light but dark things such as jealousy, inferiority or anger. These secondary group processes also need representation, for they, too, are leaders in creating the field. They usually stay in the background and confound the efforts of the foreground roles to accomplish things.

All roles which polarize and create a field are leadership roles; all are essential, because without one of them, the field cannot express itself. This knowledge gives us a special detachment, understanding and compassion towards people. Even the role of the silent one is a leadership role; it is where the heart and the dreamer usually live.

Sorting out the Different Roles

As group process work is beginning, many individuals will want to speak up. These many voices are analogous to the many signals experienced by an individual. Which signals we follow depends upon the way we sort them out. In an individual, there are primary signals which are intended, providing information about known problems or given difficulties. Likewise a group may present an agenda of problems to be worked out. Some problems may be grouped together; many apparently different feelings usually sort themselves out into two, three, four or five different roles. I have never seen a group with more than five different opinions. A good facilitator notices that individual need, and ideas can be grouped under one of these roles.

Intervening

Once the roles are identified, the facilitator creates positions in the room for each role, and asks those who feel like those roles to fill them by standing there. This intervention merely outlines the field; it structures the interactions so that they can occur; it breaks up the feeling of stasis; and it briefly disrupts the status quo, therefore requiring just a bit of courage. Group work respects the status quo and also the background field.

Encountering

Once the roles are identified, they can consciously meet one another and the process can begin. Until now, the field was simply present, like a static state, an information float. Now it begins to flow and evolve.

Do the different parts know one another? Good facilitators would first imagine their way into the role and interact from there, using their own intuition and feeling to find out how the representatives of each role would talk, act, what they would say, and what they would think of the other roles in the field. It is useful to use different parts of a room to give the roles physical locations and to allow the people playing the roles to interact. Ask others to help fill out these roles. Allowing the tension to differentiate itself into different roles is an intervention which gives the field a chance to express itself.

The Polycephalous Individual

One reason why most of us avoid public life and avoid playing leading roles is because our nature is more complex than any given role. An individual has many parts, and thus feels identified with many roles, not just one. It is limiting for an individual to stay identified with one specific role for a long time.

In processing the group field, people do not have to take only one role, but are free to change roles. This intervention creates a sort of improvisational theatre, contrasting with a more conventional theatre which rehearses first and then dramatizes world issues.

I worked once in a group in which a woman said she was angry at another participant for his sexual encounters. The room froze in silence. Sex was a taboo subject and everyone was frightened that the subject had been broached. My staff brought out the tension by depicting a figure on one side of the room who was afraid of saying things in public. Another side of the room was given to a sexually free figure, while a third side was allotted to the angry one. The room was spatially segmented in roles as follows:

Sexual Freedom ★   ★ Repression and Anger

★

Shyness and Fear

Roles in a Group Field

As the figures began to interact with one another, a wild encounter ensued. No one simply observed; everyone in the group was involved, except the shy ones, of course. Speakers rose spontaneously to fill roles as the tension expressed itself. After a short time, the initial conflict was transformed, the shy ones began to express their fear of conflict and the roles fell away as the field melted into a spontaneous circle, expressing a warm feeling of sadness that the roles had been so rigid and dogmatic.

If tension is given a chance to create and express itself, it dreams itself to conclusion. What seems to start out as a difference of opinion, a tension or a feeling of discomfort, almost always ends up creating a new and unpredictable collective centre, a numinous community experience.

The Silent Spirit

Those who do not speak are like the dream which has not yet happened. They are essential because they predict the future of a group. One way to think about the people who do not speak out is to understand them as the silent majority, the large number of people who do not express their opinions – those who do not vote in elections.

The silent feelings which cannot or are not yet ready to express themselves determine the future. The silent people can be brought into the field by asking someone simply to stand silently, or, if they want to, to move, speak, or dance.

In one group, some pacifists argued with a group of officers from the military. A participant just stood silently by, looking on. Finally, after fifteen minutes or so, the silent one suddenly spoke up and expressed some feelings which pulled the two groups together. The silent spirit feels many things; it feels and senses the direction which the process needs to take. At another time, in another setting, the silent ones represented the spirit of the earth, which welcomed both sides of the conflict. The silent one may be afraid, or may want to facilitate.

The one in the silent position often suffers. Many silent people are like the Maple Sprouts who resist the Firestones, mentioned in Chapter 6. They are a part of the group that suffers from the haste and fire of the main speakers, who courageously and unconsciously blast other speakers without realizing that their forcefulness hurts others because of its one-sidedness.

The silent spirit, the vocal majority, the voices in tensions, all create and process the anthropos' life. Since theatre of one sort or another is part of every group's life, process theatre is cross-cultural, and needs adaptation to the dramatic rituals of a given culture. Until now, my colleagues and I have successfully experimented with this form of process work on all major continents.

Identifying Different Process Modes

A global approach to people perceives various secondary ways in which we express ourselves.

Dreams

The group spirit and its issues may appear in night-time dreams. I remember one group which could not find peace until a participant dreamed that the group needed more time to feel things. When we enacted this dream, many strong feelings came out. I think of Black Elk's dreams and the way they helped the Indians to find a new tribal centre (see Picture 13, Black Elk's Tribal Centre).

Gossip

Field problems appear in the gossip outside and inside the group meetings. Close friends gossip when they get together in the pauses, expressing things which would be forbidden in the group. Gossip done with awareness can be offered to the 'garbage pail' or enacted directly in the main group.

Individuals' Difficulties

The problems of a group may appear in individuals who seem to have many problems. When a field is constantly disturbed by someone's problems, this person may represent important needs for everyone to process. This person can also be comprehended as the identified patient, the scapegoat or the representative of minority opinion.

I remember a man who continually interrupted the group, and excused his interruptions by claiming that he was schizophrenic. When everyone picked up his position and started interrupting each other and hallucinating, not only did he laugh and feel better, but the rest of the group became more creative. Was he mad or were the others insufficiently creative?

Body Problems

Problems may appear in the body symptoms of a member. One

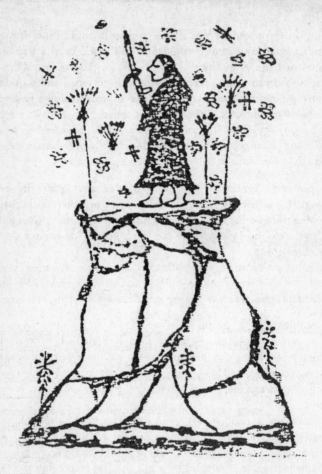

13. Black Elk's Tribal Centre

fundamentalist group was discussing how to deal with evil among its members, when suddenly a woman in the back doubled over in pain. After work on her cramps, she discovered a god-like figure who wanted to have more freedom. That brought a solution to the group's problem.

Many-levelled Work

Group work requires a global, many-levelled approach to people. Whether to use dreams, personal conflicts, relationships, gossip, or body symptoms depends upon the group process. At a given moment a large group will need to break up and work on problems in smaller groups, and at another moment small-group work cannot proceed because the issues must be solved by the entire forum.

Ideology:

Identifying and Respecting the Group Ideology

Being sensitive to the group's identity and communicating with it through its own language, ideology and belief system is a useful intervention. This idea is as ancient as the adage, 'When in Rome, do as the Romans do.'

If one uses the language and ideology of the primary process, even unwanted and disturbing behaviour or ideas can be presented in an acceptable way. For example, a family which identifies itself as being communicative and loving has trouble with an extremely introverted daughter. The therapist, by valuing the members' open communication, makes them feel happy, and is then able to formulate the shy daughter's behaviour as her particular form of open communication. The therapist can justify giving the daughter permission to go to her room using the family members' ideology, by explaining to them that there are many ways of doing the same thing. The wisest facilitator realizes that just as each individual person has her own nature, groups too are individuals and want to be respected. Learning to appreciate the ideologies and the individual nature of given groups has been very important to me personally. Realizing that a group is also a person requiring acceptance has opened me up to love people in unexpected ways.

Networking:

Identifying and Working with Network Methods

Group-process facilitation depends upon understanding how a community identifies itself and which modes of communication it prefers and unconsciously uses. For example, a group may speak of the need for greater vision, yet there is a sad feeling in the atmosphere. Hence, working with some combination of feelings (their secondary mode) and visions or dreams (their primary one) could be helpful.

Channel Switching

Getting stuck communicating can sometimes be relieved by switching channels. Since most people use their outer vision, looking internally and using inner vision might be useful. I recall a group of people that was told to see the atmosphere as a dream. They saw the other group members as animals, and fantasized into their movements, imagining them doing things they had not actually done.

Feeling and making visualizations of these feelings, moving what we are seeing, listening and then visualizing what we hear, are specific channel-switching interventions. Most people can, with a little encouragement, make up a fairy tale about their personal or collective predicament.

People need lots of room for creativity and often resist being identified with a given negative or positive role. This is not just due to fear, but to the need to live out all sides of our personality. A fluid individual will need to play many roles. Roles remain the same, but people need the freedom to switch in order to be whole and to allow the field to express itself. (However, when all the roles have been expressed, the concept of roles must fall away so that everyone is allowed to be who they are as individual people.)

Role switching is especially necessary when people are being used as scapegoats. Helping the scapegoat with his or her role is necessary, because the scapegoat is a group channel. Each role is a channel for the group to express its myth. For an individual to identify only with one channel, whether the disturber, leader, healer, spirit or evil one, is an inflation. No one person can be any one role; he or she can only occupy it temporarily.

Body Experiences

When physical tension, fatigue or uneasiness are mentioned, allowing these tensions to express themselves is helpful if the facilitators are knowledgeable in this kind of bodywork. (We must consider the possibility that fatigue arises because a group has missed an edge or important point.)

I worked once with a group which was interrupted by the owner of the hotel complaining that the participants were too noisy. After the owner had left, we used role-play to imagine the owner as part of the group. Soon the field channel switched; we no longer expressed ourselves in terms of the owner but became aware of a feeling of discomfort in the room. We began to work individually on body-oriented experiences, and the room became very quiet. By switching to body experiences, the field could integrate the owner who wanted us to be quiet.

Movement Work

When people get up, move around, leave the room, or seem agitated and cannot speak, movement as a means of expressing the tension is very useful.[1] Some things can only be expressed through movement. Movement is usually the least used form of expression in the Western world and one we need to learn about. If there is not enough room for everyone to move around, just working with the movement of one person, or the movements of one side of the room can be very helpful. A group polarized into two sides would be helped by being allowed to enact the polarization physically: first they should stand on two sides of a room and then they should switch sides, ending up on the opposite side of the room. (They would experience this movement as a powerful breakthrough in the group dynamic.)

Divining the World Spirit

Many people in both ancient and modern times have used divination procedures such as the *I Ching* to ask the world spirit to speak to them. When the process–work group in Zurich was first forming, we did not know much about group processing and asked the *I Ching* to advise us. The hexagram we got was 'Work on What Has Been Spoiled'. If we had known better about working with group processes, we would have taken its good advice and worked on the issue of forming a new institution by enacting the polarization through role-play, with some members supporting the old institution and others supporting the new one in the group. We might even have discovered that the personality of the old institution could be found in the new one as well. A more personal way of divining the global spirit is to 'spin the pen', and let it point to one member of a group arranged in a circle. This person's process is then the group's 'Tao', a channel of the field.

I remember that the pen once pointed to a woman who had terrible money problems. She was so poor that she wanted to sneak out of paying her rent in the village where the seminar was being held. But this was a global problem! Money was the last thing the group wanted to talk about. She discovered that her money problems had the function of bringing her closer to the people in the village where the seminar was held. Her problems made her relate to others by forcing her to ask them for financial help. It was amazing how her problems then allowed everyone else in the room to contact the money problems in their lives.

Relationship

A couple that disturbs a group because they cannot solve their personal problems is a symptom of a relationship problem in the whole group. It seems as if the world leaders who have chronic relationship trouble are doing something so that all of us can wake up. Instead of focusing upon the troubled couple, each of us should work on our own relationship problems.

Auditory Interventions

Groups can also be characterized by their sound. Some groups are silent. It could be that they are listening for something not yet said. Other groups make a lot of noise. Ask them to listen and amplify the noise. One particularly noisy group listened to themselves, amplified the sound they heard, and found that the yelling and arguing turned into a beautiful song. How surprising that the antagonists were ready to drop their viewpoints and sing together.

Noise which comes from the outside makes everyone suffer at one time or another. I remember starting to study with a group which was very stiff. Suddenly, a terrible cacophony came from trucks working outside. How relieving it was for us to pick up that noise, and to make it louder than the trucks! It was fun, helped to relieve the earlier shyness, and made us unaware of the outer noise!

Gossip

Watch for the moment when participants turn to their neighbours to whisper. Recommending that everyone gossip about what is happening brings the information in the gossip into the field.

I remember a group that started whispering after a man and woman had a physical fight in the middle of the room. How terrifying this was. No one dared to speak. After taking the time to gossip, everyone's stories of their own battles came up. All the stories depicted an abused and an angry person and we resolved this archetypal conflict through polarizing the two roles in the group.

Gossiping about group experience outside the group – trying to comprehend what occurs in a group – is one of the main spontaneous ways in which groups transform. Gossip needs time to develop! It becomes a problem only when its content is not somehow represented in the group's life.

Analysis

Groups often focus on self-analysis. When a field starts talking about itself or metacommunicating, then analysing the group network and process is called for. It would be useful to discuss with such a group its structure and process: what the primary and secondary processes are, which roles are not wanted, where the edges are, etc.

In fact, noticing, tracking and announcing the change of roles and themes in a group process can be very helpful. This kind of 'updating' analysis enables everyone to step out and consciously follow, especially when processes are difficult, painful or chaotic.

However, analysis and objective commenting must come from the group's heart otherwise such analysis can be detrimental to feeling experiences.

Awareness:

Understanding Primary and Secondary Processes

Interventions of awareness are based on the understanding that groups have a primary process – issues and ideologies with which they identify – and a secondary process, consisting of that which happens to them with which they do not want to identify. Most primary processes are connected with issues. The secondary ones are usually emotional, concerned with hurt, happiness, power needs and spiritual requirements, all of which the group has an edge against.

The primary process is the sense of 'we' which members refer to, the thing which makes the family or group different from others. It could be a common interest in bowling, a religious agreement, or a professional connection. A city's local environment or a nation's myth may be primary. Working on the primary process of identity can help people find out what it really means to be Chinese, American, German, Israeli, African, Hawaiian, Californian, Protestant, environmentalist or a jogger.

The primary process of a group may be identified with an individual, for example, a president who manifests a belief or ideology and who provides a means of processing secondary material. The secondary process contains the other feelings and goals which do not fit the primary ideology: egotism, power and jealousy.

Becoming Aware of Signals, Feedback and Feelings

Flip-flopping

Groups, like individuals, tend to forget their ideologies and identities when dealing with emotional issues. Thus the most dignified group of people will find such pleasure in getting angry that they will forget their primary ideals. First there is a resistance against being angry, yet once they find their anger, they have a new resistance against being calm again. This flip-flop process is why we frequently avoid emotional issues in the first place. We know that if we get into them we may lose our way and not return.

Feedback

Groups need encouragement to try something new. But you must be congruent with them to encourage them. If you are uncertain of the intervention you are recommending, the individual and group will be too. (However, if you mention your uncertainty, you are again congruent with the group and the intervention might be picked up, especially if uncertainty is in the group field.)

Negative feedback to an intervention is characterized by a lack of enthusiasm and energy. If the facilitator's intervention does not get picked up by the group, it should be dropped. I once recommended to a group that they meditate on their silence. After five minutes I asked them what they had experienced but no one answered. They were asleep! This was negative feedback. They needed time to gossip about what had been happening, not meditate on it.

Working with Altered States; Recognizing the Drive for Wholeness; Picking up Group Projections

People need altered states and the depth of experience that goes with them. One reason why we tend to avoid group life is because its superficial focus leaves out deeper, spiritual experiences. (Another reason for avoiding groups can be the opposite, because we fear the altered states which they pull us into.) Global awareness means appreciating and working with the altered states that groups, like individuals, need for life. This is, after all, why we create rituals, dances, plays and musical festivals.

Most rituals create altered states by changing channels: the primary process of the group, its issues, beliefs and talk are left, and channels not normally used, such as music or movement, are focused on. Old and established rituals would be more meaningful if they did not merely leave out or ignore the issues of the primary process, but transformed them by bringing them into new channels.

Knowing which channels are occupied and which are unoccupied can help facilitate a group situation. Unoccupied channels bring fields together by expressing their core and expanding their experience. For example, a group which has been talking a lot can experience an incredible coming together if one member merely mentions a dream (switching from auditory to visual channels); this entirely reorganizes the group experience by giving it a new pattern. Or, to take another example, a group which has just felt something wonderful could sense even more completely what has happened by not just feeling it, but by making pictures, movements and sounds which express the experience.

Asking a talkative field to be quiet creates an altered state. A silent, introverted group may enter an altered state simply by greeting one another. Asking an academic or professional group to use their unoccupied body feeling can stimulate wonders.

I remember doing body work with people from the US Air Force. One of the officers wanted help with a backache and when I placed my hand on his back so that he could feel it more, he discovered that fear was located there. He said suddenly that he was shy about expressing his fear, since fear was not allowed in the military. Then in the night, he dreamed that the US withdrew its troops from Europe because they were no longer needed. He told us, almost crying, that if we were all allowed to express our fear of hurting and being hurt, we could all withdraw our defences since they would no longer be needed.

But body feeling may be a group's primary process, while relationships might contain the group's altered state. I remember once working with a yoga group which transformed its field by ironing out its relationship problems. An encounter group may have an occupied relationship channel, but may be unconnected to the world.

A group whose primary process wants to keep everything impersonal will enter into a strong altered state if one person tells a personal story. It is important to remember that such altered experiences are due to our drive to be whole; individuals and groups want access to all of their channels, processes and feelings.

Garbage:

Dealing with Repressed Issues and Information Float

Because a group cannot express everything publicly, creating a recycling can for unwanted feelings and ideas is an essential and interesting intervention. Which contents a group processes from the can depends upon the field.

An entire book should be devoted to the public's need for the dark side of life.[2] I will content myself here with encouraging the world to learn how to process difficult issues, because this is where the gold lies. The alchemists knew about finding gold. They knew that in the midst of human misery and pain, in the midst of chaos, which they called the 'prima materia' – the raw material of life – was gold.

The dark side of ourselves shows us the parts of life we are shy about. It throws us into tumultuous, non-equilibrium processes. Though it confuses and scares us, it also breaks down barriers and reunites people in unbelievable ways. Forbidden issues knock us off our old centres and press us to open up to the whole of life. Such processes always demonstrate the incredible wisdom hidden in the field of the anthropos. The Jungians are correct to say that the way to the Self is through the Shadow. The global mind uses impossible issues to reveal its divine centre.

Chapter Twelve

War Games and Conflict Methods

The possibility of another world war is so real that scarcely a day passes without our reading about it in the newspapers or thinking about it. We all know that another world war could be the last, yet we are at a loss as to how to stop it.

It seems possible to me that if we don't learn how to transform the energy of conflict and war into more creative processes, we will make human life obsolete. Like the gods in the Götterdämmerung, it appears, at first inspection, that human beings can do nothing to stop their own destruction.

Picture 14 shows the statue of St Michael and the Devil standing near the entrance to Coventry Cathedral. This statue symbolizes the resurgence of the good over the evil forces of the enemy. Yet if we look closely at this picture, we see that St Michael has a pointed spear, just as the Devil has pointed horns. The pointedness of the Devil does not disappear, but appears in the form of the victor's weapon. This picture inadvertently implies that one cannot conquer evil; it has not been transformed, only copied by the conqueror.

By the 1950s, Europe was well on its way to economic recovery. Prominent Nazis were being tried for their war crimes at Nuremberg, and the world seemed to be getting back in order. Picture 15, Trial of War Criminals at Nuremberg, again depicts the Devil (now in the form of German leaders) bound. Thus, for example, it is possible to kill people, but not a role; the 'Devil' in the form of tyranny and violence is still with us. The attempt to enforce law by the victors is another such paradoxical scheme. Look at how the old scores of tyranny were settled in the Hungarian uprising (see Picture 16). The prisoner under escort in that picture was probably an official of the overthrown regime. Could we say the Devil had been overthrown, or was he merely unconsciously projected? It is difficult to see in this picture, and in many similar situations, who is the evil dictator and who is the victim.

Why Guns?

By developing the machine gun, we hoped to make cavalry charges obsolete. Likewise, we thought the atomic bomb would make war obsolete. Today, 400 nuclear weapons would be required to eliminate the United States and the Soviet Union. Why, then, did the United States make 50,000 nuclear weapons in 1986? They do not rescue hostages from terrorists, keep the Soviets out of Afghanistan or the Third World free of Communism.

If the fascination with weapons is so great, it must be due to the fact that we need more of them in some way. We need them psychologically! We have more than enough war machines, but too little knowledge of how to process personal conflicts. In working on our conflicts in a useful way, most of us have come no further than our cave-dwelling ancestors whose fight repertoire was limited to fight or flight techniques.

War Games

At a seminar on conflict resolution for The Colorado Institute for Conflict Resolution and Creative Leadership (CICRCL), I introduced a war game to give people an experimental grasp of global conflict. This experiment turned out to be the most educational shock I have yet had about war.[1] The theory I wanted to test and was able to prove was: no one wants conflict; we try to forget it, thereby inadvertently propagating a war for which we are unprepared. The one-hundred-member study group decided to process the US conflict with Iran that was happening in the Persian Gulf at that time, 4 October 1987. The game was set up as follows: six people standing in a line represented the US leaders, and six standing in an opposing line, the Iranians.

Behind these two groups were another two groups of twenty people

14. St Michael and the Devil

15. *Nuremberg Trial of War Criminals*

16. The Hungarian Uprising

who were not allowed to speak during the proceedings, but were
encouraged to make noises representing the collective opinion behind
the leaders. The rest of us sat on the sides and watched.

There were no further instructions about what should happen. The
longer the US and Iranian leaders debated, the louder the two background groups representing collective opinion became. By making so
much noise, they boisterously pressed their leaders closer and closer to

War Game

confrontation. Finally and out of the blue, as the two front lines of the groups moved closer to one another, some unknown participant ran forward, yelling above the noise that he would drop a bomb. No one paid attention to him in the midst of the chaos and so he dropped the bomb, made a huge noise and the 'world' blew up. The groups confronted and intermingled as the bomb went off, playing out the national collectives which had driven the countries to war as the rest of the world stood by and watched.

After the World had Ended

Surprisingly, after the 'bomb' had exploded, everyone simply lay on the floor, 'dead', strewn haphazardly on top of each other. The room was absolutely quiet. No one spoke. After what seemed hours, several voices began whispering, asking what had happened. Instead of discussing the game in the large group, the field broke up and each worked individually and internally on his or her most difficult conflict by writing a dialogue between the different sides of the conflict. Using the idea of Jung's active imagination, the participants tried to slow down the internal escalation of their own conflicts in order to process all sides.[2]

The next morning, we were surprised to learn that in the night there had been a real battle between the US and Iran in the Middle East. I have frequently seen such synchronicities, in which a group event mirrored an outer event. Are such events evidence of the non-local behaviour of global fields?

In any case, several people spoke that morning about their war-game experience and many questions were asked. Why was there such a love of murder? Why did everyone, soldiers and pacifists alike, get so excited about playing war? A few of the pacifists who had participated in the game were shocked, and courageously admitted that they had been excited by the game's violence and killing, an excitement which they had never experienced before. Of course, this was just a game. Yet, why was it thrilling to be so angry and aggressive? There are innumerable reasons for aggression, some of which have already been discussed in this book. But another reason worth thinking about is that we forbid ourselves to be angry in our personal lives.

Since anger and murder are allowed on a national basis it becomes a thrilling relief to be allowed to be angry and kill in the name of the flag. The world encourages murder and the altered states of aggression and pain in the name of nationalism. These states are forbidden to us as individuals. This is one of the reasons why we so often find ourselves at war. Even those in the game who believed in their sanity had to question their actions and behaviour.

Group Altered States

How rapidly a group of well-meaning people was transformed into a wild and dangerous organization! Once a field leaves its boring primary process behind, any altered state, even aggression, feels like freedom. Witness a rock concert or a political meeting. When a group flips, it leaves its old centre, its homeostasis and rationality behind.[3]

And what about death? Why was it so pleasant to die in the war game? Death was a relief after the wild aggression. Death is a chance to quieten down and find a new centre; it is a short cut back to a peaceful state and an end to the madness. We need to learn how to die more constructively, to drop out and go inside ourselves with consciousness during a conflict.

And what about the passive audience? Why didn't the audience intervene in the 'war'? In real life, also, there are far too few who are responsible for the bomb, and far too many who just watch. The audience forgets their fear, imagining that war could not happen. Everyone hopes that someone else will do something.

We forget that our dreams and feelings are part of the momentary field. Our individual experiences are important! The physics of non-locality and the field of the collective unconscious imply that our personal lives are global. When the time is urgent, the concepts of inside and outside, of individual and globe must disappear as the courage to intervene in world events grows. In a world of nonlocality, we must remember that there is no way out – unconsciousness does not work, nor even does death. We can kill our bodies, but not our roles or fields. In a sense, war and death are illusions, since they solve nothing.

Conflict Training

So let's drop nuclear weapons and pick up other things which will satisfy us even more, the tools to enter relationship conflicts in which both parties win.

Most conflict has focused upon physical combat traditionally used by men. Let's develop a modern method which accepts physical fighting as only a minor component in conflict resolution.

To develop our process-oriented conflict methods, we should think about the actual experiences we have in battle. Most experts agree upon the following characteristics of long-standing conflicts.

Symmetrical Projections

In battle we project identical things on to one another. Research shows that both the Americans and the Soviets feel that:

a. The other side is an aggressor.
b. The other's government exploits and deludes the people.

   c. The mass of people on the other side are not really sympathetic
      to their regime.
   d. The other side cannot be trusted.
   e. The policy of the opposing side verges on madness.[4]

If both parties agree on these projections, then these beliefs create the
information floating in the air. Our global atmosphere is composed of
aggression, delusion, revolution, mistrust and madness. These projections are ideas we all have about our enemies. We secretly or not so
secretly believe that our enemies are aggressive, that they delude
themselves about the truth, that their friends do not really like them,
and that they cannot be trusted because they are just a little bit crazy.

Global Fear of Altered States

Fear is a reason why we hesitate to clear the atmosphere. We avoid
conflict, and mistrust our own aggression, believing that if we get
angry, someone will get hurt or lose their mind. The worst danger of
aggression is that if we get angry, we might not be able to find our
way back to our ordinary selves.

    Thus we avoid our aggression and project it on to the enemy. We
mistrust our enemy because we think his emotions and altered states
are unpredictable. We mistrust his anger because we cannot trust our
own aggression. In fact, we should not trust either our own or our
neighbour's altered states. We can trust only that which we know.
When people get angry, they are different. Anger temporarily changes
a person's identity and usually makes her forget everyone else. Though
the world tells us to trust more, I recommend not trusting anyone in
an altered state, either yourself or your enemies, unless you are familiar
with the altered state.

I. Using Avoidance in Conflict

Thus, the first step in conflict-resolution training is to become aware of
the natural processes of mistrust which make us avoid altered states.

Let me ask a question about aggression. When you see two animals fighting or killing each other, you may feel badly but you are not angry with them. When you see the ocean crashing upon the rocks, you do not get angry with the ocean, though you know it is 'killing' the shoreline. Why do we get so angry when people fight?

One reason is that we identify with only one side of human conflicts, attach ourselves to either the attacker or victim and lose the feeling of the detached observer. Our attachment to one side and loss of detachment scares us and makes us avoid conflict.

These are the first two steps in working with conflict: avoid it, and avoid identifying with only one side. Conflict work begins with being afraid, avoiding the fight, mistrusting our altered states, and waiting until we can identify with all the parts in combat.

To create a detached position from which to enter the conflict later, we need to work with our altered states, with our fears, anger, dizziness and rage. Afterwards, we shall be able to enter into conflict and process events to a rich conclusion for all.

II. Inner Work on Conflict

Remember: this section is designed to facilitate working internally on our behaviour in a conflict. Do you recall a current or past personal conflict? Take a look at yourself. Are you the aggressor or the victim in the conflict? Perhaps you are both. Can you find out what started it?

Feel: note the feelings you have about your opponent. Feel them and watch yourself feeling them. Can you see yourself having these feelings? Do you feel fear, anger or sadness? What do you look like having these feelings?

Withdraw: if you are feeling afraid of your opponent or yourself, then be afraid. Withdraw, and keep pulling away, watching yourself do so, until you find a safe place, perhaps thousands of miles away from the conflict. It's important that you take your fear seriously. Withdraw, and understand that you may be withdrawing in order to leave the scene, so that you can find an objective point, outside the emotional field, to help you get an overview of the situation.

Anger: if you are angry, watch yourself expressing it and tell your opponent why you are angry and what you really want. If you are sad, then express this, too, to your opponent.

If you do these things completely, the conflict may be resolved for you internally. If it is, that is fine. If not, the next step is to meditate upon your opponent.

The Opponent: look at your enemy from a distance, watching and monitoring closely. Listen closely. What do you hear and see? You might notice something you have not noticed before. Observe yourself and your opponent together. What sort of ideas or feelings do you get now looking at the two of you?

Help the Opponent: since this is only an inner-work exercise, why not help your opponent to express and do what she needs to? Help her come out even more directly with what she wants. If you can, feel your way into her state of mind and guess how she must be feeling. Though this is difficult, try it and you will understand her psychology better. As you feel your way into her state of mind, imitate her movements and find out when you behave as she does. Do you sometimes act and move like your enemy?

The Opponent's Attack: let your enemy attack you and watch her do it. Do not fight, but use her energy. Surprise her and catch her off guard by agreeing with her attacks. Find out what part of her attack is justified and what part is not. You will recognize in this conflict meditation a way of working with your own inner criticism. This is important work for all of us.

Open Up to the Opponent: try accepting her viewpoint. Is this viewpoint very difficult for you to accept? Is it disturbing for you? What would it mean for you to change in her direction? Could her viewpoint be at all useful to you?

Work with a Helper: now that you have worked internally on the conflict, it might be educational to play out the conflict with someone who is not the opponent. Experiment with the steps which you used on yourself. Tell your friend how to behave as your enemy. Step away from the conflict, look at it, ask your friend to play you and at another time to play the opponent. Step out and go back in, even helping the opponent to attack, playing the opponent yourself, experimenting with slowing or speeding up all movements. Then try to use the attack she gives you; this is a type of aikido. Step back and look at yourself and your opponent.

This procedure certainly helps to process inner conflicts and may also obviate the outer work. It is useful training for working with projections, developing detachment, and becoming aware of the different roles we play in conflict.

A Warning: be careful about avoiding outer conflicts. Though you can momentarily change yourself with an inner-work procedure, development also depends on working on relationships in the world. Using only inner work as a solution will not hold. So take the time and energy and set up a meeting to find out more about relationship work.[5]

III. Training in Altered States

We are usually unprepared for relationship problems and fall into an altered state the moment we confront difficult emotions and states such as anger, fear and aggression. Thus, working on our dark corners is good preparation for handling conflict. Think of the most difficult emotional conflict you have had.

1. Write down a description of this state.
2. Then act this state out or see yourself acting it out without completely feeling it.
3. Is it hard to act? What do you dislike about this part of yourself?
4. Make a picture out of this state. See yourself. Are you frozen or blocked?
5. Now experiment with this state. Let it unfold all the way. Try doing this with someone else or watch yourself doing it alone.
6. Can you hear yourself making noises or speaking? Listen to what you say. Say it completely.
7. Take the focus away from your opponent, or whoever has caused this emotional state, and just speak your message to the world.
8. Find out if there is a simple statement about your needs which you have not yet brought out.

One reason why people get blocked in relationship conflicts is that they do not allow themselves to feel or bring out the above emotions, statements or needs. They think they are too infantile, unfitting, or crazy. Experiment with changing your self-image until it corresponds to the emotions and needs in the background. Maintaining an image in which there is no place for emotions will freeze you into an altered state whenever you get into a conflict. One way to understand conflict is to understand that it forces us to integrate the feelings behind our altered states into our self-image.

When you feel you have finished working internally and have become fluid enough to enter altered states and leave them again, go on. Use your self-awareness and meet your opponent.

IV. Training in Double Signals and Self-Knowledge

What are your goals in a conflict? An important goal for me is to learn about myself, about my opponent and to help us both 'win'. An aikido master once said that no one can win a fight unless both are enlightened. In order for me to be enlightened, I need to be clearer about who I am.

Interrupt conflicts by asking yourself questions about your emotional state. Train yourself to become aware in a conflict by asking yourself during the interaction:

What does my voice sound like as I speak?
What incomprehensible body motions do I make?
Which people or issues do I mention that are absent?
Which body feelings do I have that I am not bringing into the discussion?
Which dreams or fantasies do I try to avoid?
What is happening in the environment, which I have been neglecting?

The answer to these questions will tell you about the kinds of unconscious processes you need to use in the conflict. Your unconscious or 'double' signals will help resolve conflicts rapidly and meaningfully, enlightening you about who you are, and deepening your interactions. Try these questions while working with a friend. Then meet your opponent over a cup of tea and clean up the atmosphere for us all.

One divorced couple worked on their relationship recently during a period of thirty minutes. He yelled that she asked too much of him, and she courageously admitted that it was true, she had wanted even more. In fact, she found him too unpredictable! He accepted this and then said that the most unpredictable thing he could do right now was to say that she had been the centre and meaning of his life. At that moment, they discovered the centre of their interaction and recreated a new meaning in their relationship.

Their conflict ended in a deepened relationship. But the moral of the story lies in their history. They were able to process such painful and difficult tension clearly and rapidly because both of them had previously worked on their own altered states and trained in conflict resolution.

Chapter Thirteen

The Year I

Within UNCTAD, the United Nations Council for Trade and Development, paralysis and immobilization have characterized conflict negotiations between the richer northern nations and the poorer ones of the South.[1] The kernel of the Third World, the so-called group of seventy-seven, unites just long enough to ask for a reduction in its debt, but cannot unite long enough to ask for anything else. The Third World countries gather only because of the troubled global economic scene, not because of their good feeling for one another. They join because of the role they play in the global field.

UNCTAD tends to side with the poorer Third World against the richer industrialized nations of the North because of their apparent relative weakness. There is so much internal fighting among the Third World nations that they cannot congruently stand for their own cause. UNCTAD describes the situation:

> The main question at issue is whether it is proper for international civil servants to render assistance to one particular group of countries by helping it to define its objectives, and subsequently to bring pressure on other groups for cooperation in achieving those objectives.[2]

The former Secretary-General of the United Nations, U Thant, and his assistants, Paul Prebisch and W. R. Malinowski, felt that they were following the letter of the UN charter in supporting the Third World countries against the North. Thant thought he was taking

> due account of the fact that some nations were much weaker than others, and much less well-equipped to argue their own case before the organs of the United Nations . . . in a television interview with

Ambassador Adlai Stevenson ... [U Thant] said that it was very difficult for a UN official to be neutral on the burning issues of the day. Whoever occupied the office of Secretary-General must be impartial, ... but not necessarily neutral.[3]

UNCTAD argued that they were adhering to the policy of the United Nations World Health Organization. Like WHO, they could not be neutral relative to difficult issues of the day and had to do whatever they could to 'solve the problems of ill-health and under-development'.

There is no doubt that the [resulting] fierce opposition of the OECD countries to ... [the UN] made it very difficult at times for the UNCTAD staff to retain the confidence of these countries and hence to function as effectively as they might as mediators in the clash of views between North and South.[4]

The UN meddled in a global process by taking sides and could have created war, in a more volatile world situation. The UN acted as any loving neighbour would to protect the apparent weakest in a powerful family where the weak one could not hold his own against the strong.

On Weak and Strong

However humanitarian and just the concepts of weak and strong may be, they are outmoded, limited, non-global concepts. In a global field, each role is an essential part, critical for the very existence of the field. In an absolute sense, there can be no stronger or weaker party in a fight, because strong and weak are two equally powerful roles.

Nations and roles are not identical. Any nation could just as easily play a weak or strong role. Weak and strong are relative concepts. Since 75 per cent of the world consists of the 'poorer' Third World, we could just as easily imagine them to be the strong ones, based on their sheer size alone. Strong and weak are roles which nations must play at a given moment.

Not only the identified 'weak' are weak. In a process sense, weak refers to a lack of awareness, because those who inadvertently attach themselves to one role or get lost in an altered state from which they cannot return, are in a 'weak' position. They now become victims of life instead of creating it. Likewise, a facilitator, such as the UN, which loses its global viewpoint and supports or identifies with one part is weakened, and like any beginner in conflict resolution, creates more conflict than necessary by confusing party with role. With more experience, the global facilitator learns to feel and support the entire field, siding with the whole, as much as with any of its parts.

Everyone in conflict needs help; we are all weak and troubled in such a situation. Since we are the only facilitators on our tiny planet, the safest position is to fight for the side we believe in but also for the life of the whole and to be open to communications from the other side. We must stand for the whole because only when all the parts are able to express themselves can the whole operate humanely and wisely. We need to realize that our tendency to take sides and forget the whole injures it.[5]

The global field does not work when only one side is supported, even though the tendency to favour only one part is real and important. There are no absolute good or bad parts in a relativistic field; absolute 'good' or 'evil' are feelings of only one side. Believing that one of the roles in conflict is 'good' is naïve and siding only with what we believe to be the 'good' side disturbs the whole, or even worse, can bring on world war. We need to learn to support the side we believe in and simultaneously support the entire system just as much.

Historians warn us through modern global myths of the suicide, life and death of civilizations:

> The history of the world before AD1500 has a certain pattern. It shows civilizations succeeding each other, repeating each other, perhaps improving upon each other. But the basic character of these civilizations remains comparable. Moreover, the world has room for all of them. But from about AD1500 we can trace a profound change in world history. From that date we find one civilization, European civilization, developing and displaying a new and unique character, and, thanks to that character, imposing itself on the whole world. Whatever the future may hold, this change is permanent. The world is now united as never before; and it is united, even after

the European empires have passed away, by irreversible European ideas and techniques.[6]

Thus, since 1500, the world has been organized by European ideas. Today, the Third World hardly realizes the wisdom and value of its own ancient traditions as it strives to assimilate Western technology.

Europe, however, has been not only the perpetrator of imperialist and colonialist policies, but also the creator of humanitarian sentiments.

In a political sense it is still proper to date the age in which we live from the French Revolution. The shock carried by that revolution and the spread of its principles has produced repercussions ever since. They will continue today, whenever people claim the rights of national self-determination and of equality before the law. The social history of France, and Europe too, was permanently changed by the institutions set up when the Third Estate seized power and turned the States General into the National Assembly . . .

So when on the 21 September 1792 the members of the Convention believed that they were justified in dating that 'moment' as the Year I, they may be said to have marked, if not the beginning of the contemporary world, at least the opening of a revolutionary phase in history, a point from which continual change became a normal fact of human existence.[7]

The Year I, symbolizing the moment when all people and roles are accepted as equal, is still a dream trying to happen. The Year I really stands for more than the French Revolution; it represents all efforts, from the American Revolution to the French Revolution and right up to modern revolutions and movements that strive to realize the importance and freedom of the individual.

Preceding these revolutions, the primary process of the Western world was characterized by feudalism, the wealth of the clergy, social inequality determined by the elite minority, and rulership by a king who had little understanding of the needs of the people. The American and French Revolutions intended to overthrow despotism and to give people self-determination. These revolutions attempted to end inequality and to replace it with the 'rights of man' as the guiding concept for the new constitutions.

The Year I

But the meaning of the 'rights of man', or rather, the rights of every part of the human being and human field, will be realized when we find a global approach to everyday conflicts and world problems. The Year I stands for the view that understands conflict between parts as an attempt of the whole to know itself. We shall never be able to turn such a view into another rigid programme, for no one is permanently open to all sides. Rather, the Year I represents that particular moment in time when we appreciate that all sides identify themselves as the 'light' trying to win over the 'dark', and that ideologies are not only trying to conquer others but are attempting to differentiate themselves. It is an attitude which comprehends that no one can win over someone else, since we are all part of one being. According to Toynbee,

> We are living in an age in which, for the first time in history, the whole human race, over the whole surface of our planet, is growing together into a single world-society. We have, indeed, to become a single world-family. In the atomic age, this is the only way of banishing the present danger that we may commit mass suicide. Mankind intends to survive, and therefore we are committed to following the path of unification resolutely to its goal. This is difficult for human beings, because, till now, our paramount loyalty has been given to fractions of mankind, not to mankind as a whole. We have been, first and foremost, adherents of some local nation, civilization or religion. In future, our paramount loyalty has to be transferred to the whole human race.[8]

Toynbee's universalism itself would almost be the necessary meta-ideology which we need: sections of the human race are networks with awareness, and polycephalous diversity is accepted by all. The new-world meta-ideology is rapidly becoming that of universality, unification and togetherness.

But we must not forget the garbage, too. The secondary process at the time of the French Revolution is still around today: feudalism, egotism, despotism, hierarchical power and its global counterpart, nationalism. Toynbee puts it this way;

nationalism is a disruptive force ... the issue between universalism and nationalism is one of life and death for the human race; and the victory of universalism cannot be taken for granted ...

... the distribution of human interests has been ... the preponderance of our interest in war. In later history, war plays just as prominent a part as it does in earlier histories of the Assyrians, Mongols and Aztecs.[9]

His warnings of past conflicts, sectionalism and war imply that our present global garbage bin is still overflowing with a powerful and dangerous secondary process: nationalism, the enemy which we are supposed to overcome. But we should be careful. Any ideology which forbids others is in itself sectionalistic and creates war. Any primary process, regardless of its inherent humanism, which forbids other parts becomes another patriarchal tyrant extinguishing roles such as nationalism and egotism which are not supposed to exist. It's the attitude, therefore, and not the content of the ideology which prevents or causes war.

Moments of the Year I

Sectionalism, too, would therefore have a role if the Year I were ever to arrive. But where is the Year I? It begins as the idea of the 'rights of man' and becomes an intervention which accepts the unwanted parts of ourselves and our world.

Consider, for example, Robert Muller's story in a paper called 'Proposals For a Better World Security', in which he recalls the words of Chou En Lai during Secretary-General Waldheim's visit to Peking in 1972.

I am sitting here surrounded by my advisers trying to figure out what they might be scheming against us in Moscow and in Washington. In Moscow, they are trying to figure out what Peking and Washington might be scheming against them. And they are doing the same in Washington. But perhaps in reality no one is scheming against anyone.[10]

In the Year I such scheming would be understood as the part which is being rejected and as a fantasy which must be encouraged and expressed in order to create greater connection between the leaders. The fantasies behind such scheming would probably involve destroying the others. If this scheming were openly admitted, the nationalism and ambition behind it might be reduced as the world powers awakened to the fact that they all harboured similar fantasies of destroying the planet on which they lived.

In the Year I, global facilitators would encourage leaders to reveal their fantasies in order to clear the air between the nations. In the Year I 'bad' sections of the planet, like terrorists, would not only be repressed but also integrated.

Integrating terrorism would mean that more people would experiment and risk their lives for their feelings and beliefs. Integrating a part always results in our consciously taking over the energy from that part. If we all lived out more of the terrorist's role, standing up strongly for what we believed in, we would deplete the real terrorists of their energy. Integrating the terrorist means recycling and cleaning up the atmosphere, making life more exciting and terrorism less interesting.

The Significance of Networking

Can this happen? According to systems theory,

> evolution is basically open and indeterminate. There is no goal in it, or purpose, and yet there is a recognizable pattern of development . . .
> . . . Evolution is an ongoing and open adventure that continually creates its own purpose in a process whose detailed outcome is inherently unpredictable.[11]

Systems theory may not be correct about the unpredictability of the time when the 'rights of man' will begin, but it is certainly right about our ability to create meaning and purpose. The timing of the Year I is, indeed, up to you and me.

> From the systems point of view the unit of survival is not an entity
> at all, but rather a pattern of organization adopted by an organism
> in its interactions with its environment.[12]

The essential element is our attitude towards, or rather, our awareness
of, in human terms, others. The immortal human centre is simple:
systems awareness or our way of connecting to one another. How we
relate to our inner figures, to our interpersonal relationships and to our
networks is more important and also more unconscious than we may
have realized. It is the immortal part of our world.

The message is perennial and still new. We will live in the Year I
when our world and personal processes include the role of global
awareness; when we realize that each role in the world process theatre
is a leader whose communications are urgently needed. When this
awareness occurs our inner warrior awakens even when other parts of
ourselves are in altered states of rage, love, conflict or religious ecstasy.
Then we will be able to experience and know that the whole can work
only when allowed access to each of its parts, destroyer and peacemaker,
disturber and insider.

Chapter Fourteen

The Numinous Core

The assumptions of this book have been that the world we live in is partly organized by transpersonal fields within and around us. These fields are physical and psychological. The field is organized by various forces, such as gravity, electromagnetism, weak and strong nuclear forces, and dreaming, a hitherto unrecognized power. The field has often been imagined as an anthropos figure whose development is suicidal or growth-oriented. The majority of myths portray the field as having a mind of its own, one which is awakening.

Modern concepts such as Jung's collective unconscious and Sheldrake's morphic field, as well as ancient ideas from Taoism, Buddhism and Christianity, agree on one thing: the world we live in has the potential to be a wise dreamer. But modern group work indicates that this wisdom does not operate overtly unless the field we live in is made conscious to us all. Only when all of its parts are represented and appreciated, when group edges are recognized and investigated, does the field manifest its wisdom. Until now, however, our global awareness of this field has been minimal. The vast majority of the population ignore their own and the world's problems. Most of us think that the world's problems have nothing to do with us. We believe that acute crises will be solved by people and forces outside us.

But global consciousness is increasing, too. Though we notice an increasing attempt to solve our problems with causal solutions, there is also a growing awareness that the most powerful leadership in a group is the ability to follow the processes trying to happen. The old belief that power resided in one individual is now being differentiated by new field concepts. Global consciousness is relieving; it understands that we don't all need to be conscious group facilitators all the time. We can relax too! But when we feel that the time has come, we must learn how to follow the group's escalations and de-escalations, both of which always seem to create a new centre, a community, enriching and exciting for all.

Global consciousness seems to break old communication patterns. Any form of process-oriented group work brings the electricity back to our fading interest in community life. That, of course, does not take much. But there are many times when group processing is more exciting and more productive than the murder and struggles of war! Group work done with awareness brings us closer to one another. It gives us the chance to know the 'authorities' and our 'opponents' and also to get in touch with the energy and role of the 'terrible enemy' in ourselves. In this moment, the old static and apparently irreconcilable opposites, the persecuted and persecutor, begin to melt.

I have been astounded again and again to find that people locked into frozen conflict desire, more than anything, to live in a global community. The tragedy of chronic conflict lies not only in the unabating violence and hatred, but in the repression of our need for oneness. We all search for a 'home' and are waiting for our sense of immediate family to extend to people of all races and nationalities. After working with thousands of people everywhere, I am forced to conclude that behind our racism, fear and resistance to those who are different, lies our hope for closeness.

The Numinous Community Core

Community rituals such as New Year's Day, Christmas, Thanksgiving, Solstice Festivals, Passover, and Carnival are attempts to get to the numinous core of the field we live in, a centre to which we all relate. But rituals are not enough. They are programmes which give us security and hope, and which attempt to remind us of the wondrous or divine background of our world. But they also tend to reduce our interest in finding the numinous centre of life right here and now, in the everyday problems we feel, hear about and suffer from.

Rituals need to be rediscovered and created daily in the heart of our world problems. Think of the experiences mentioned in this book. Think of how the war game ended in a powerful silence, or of how the conflict between blacks and whites was resolved in a mutual experience of love and trust. I recall processing a conflict in a large growth centre which began with almost physical violence and ended with sensitivity and love.

I remember facilitating a language conflict between German and English speakers which brought up anger and resentment between the groups about the Holocaust. I recall with amazement how the group came to a momentary resolution when one single German woman stepped forward and wept in pain because of what had happened during World War II. An American Jewish woman came forward and knelt in front of her, hugging her legs as she wept, and the two spontaneously created a statue of a goddess and her worshipper.

I have frequently seen unhappy, unstable individuals disturbing huge groups through their behaviour, and then being relieved of their torture when the group integrated their madness by becoming more lively. True, some of these groups strayed far from their status quo while integrating their disturbers. These groups showed that momentary and unusual states of chaos heal the instability of the individual while creating a true community. The group went through phases of becoming a mob and suddenly a community, finding its centre in the spiritual experiences mirrored until then only in the individual's maddest dreams.

Most of the large group experiences I have witnessed have been with normal, everyday people. Each of these groups was able to find non-ordinary states of reality, and to create numinous cores, transforming the group into a community.

Where Is It All Going?

Having seen so many of these experiences forces me to make a hypothesis. Groups, communities and even our local relationship conflicts all have one thing in common. The boredom, tensions, cold war, open conflicts, aggression and madness which amaze, hypnotize and terrify all of us *are* unconscious attempts to reveal and discover the powerful and exciting, electric and holy heart of the dreambody we live in.

How else can I explain what I recently saw in Zurich, a city governed by a religious and work ethic, a very conservative and reserved city? A large group of people had come to hear me talk about our society's addiction to the status quo. We convened in a circle after the lecture. When the participants were asked what they saw in the middle of the room, some said they saw a large flower, others imagined children playing, one saw a huge stuffed animal and all laughed.

The group decided to give form to this last fantasy by playing it out. More and more individuals rose from the circle and began to join together and created a huge, cuddly stuffed animal which slowly 'moved' around the room and cuddled the others still sitting. Out of a momentary chaos, a new world had appeared, one in which the inside cuddled the outside, and people connected through their need to love and touch.

That night, Zurich became a huge body realizing a momentary dream of relatedness, giving everyone the feeling that life was still worth living.

But people all over seem to strive for this numinous community core, even though old rituals are apparently dying out. I was shocked to discover how the tribal shamanistic healing rituals in Africa are disappearing as bush life is replaced by Western or rather, cosmopolitan civilization. But the powerful spirit which creates community experience and which once gave us all a reason for living seems indestructible.

It is true that the remaining few per cent of our planet still living in a coherent tribal community will soon become extinct as the twenty-first century begins, and yet ancient forms of shamanistic ritual continue. I'll never forget how surprised my audience in Nairobi was to hear that they were not the only ones still interested in witch-doctors but that many people in northern California either consider themselves to be healers or else have recently been healed by one! Lifestyles change, but the search for the numinous both for ourselves and our communities continues with unrelinquished passion.

The Global Facilitator in Perspective

Seen from a two- or three-thousand-year perspective, the global, multi-dimensional awareness recommended by this book is finally just another role itself asking to be fulfilled by those who are called upon to do so. This used to be the job of the shamans and priests; today it is available to everyone.

From the viewpoint of world history, global thinking is just another role in a troubled planetary field. The field is created by the tension between other essential roles, such as tyranny and democracy, the persecutor and victim, the leader and follower, the hero and villain, the wise old woman and the madman. Each part of the field is the leader; each is required to create the global field, and everyone is needed to represent the known as well as the unknown and unpopular roles in the field. Only when all the parts are known can the anthropos transform its clogged and static atmosphere into an exciting and electric community.

Today, however, in the late stages of the twentieth century, the role of the globally wise facilitator is less adequately filled than any other role, even less than the evil disturber. Thus, creating and populating the new facilitator with all of its differing viewpoints is a matter of planetary life and death. We can expect the anthropos to find its own way and create necessary and unpredictable changes once we have done our job by sensing and representing the field we live in and by sensitively and courageously filling in its roles.

Notes

Full details of works quoted can be found in the bibliography.

Chapter 2

1. Einstein, *On Peace*, p. 376.
2. Council on Environmental Quality, *The Global 2000 Report to the President*.
3. Rifkin, *Entropy*, p. 3.
4. See Capra, *The Turning Point*, and Henderson, *The Politics of the Solar Age: Alternatives to Economics*, especially chapter 13.

Chapter 3

1. Rifkin, *Entropy*.
2. Mindell, *The Dreambody in Relationships*.
3. Mindell, *River's Way*.
4. Henderson, *The Politics of the Solar Age*, especially chapter 13.
5. Rifkin, op. cit.

Chapter 4

1. For a discussion of this project see Sagan, *Cosmic Connection*.
2. Naisbitt, *Megatrends*.
3. ibid.
4. Mindell, *Dreambody*.
5. Jung, 'Synchronicity, an Acausal Connecting Principle', and Sheldrake, 'Mind, Memory and Archetype'.
6. Sheldrake, in 'Mind, Memory and Archetype', discusses the connection between morphic resonance and Jung's concept of synchronicity. He gives the example of birds of the bluetit flock drowning in milk bottles trying to drink the cream off the top. Many of these birds died from the same actions in many places simultaneously, without the possibility of communicating to each other in known ways.

7.   See Mindell, *The Dreambody in Relationships*, for a full discussion of unintended communication.

8.   ibid.

9.   Cutajar (ed.), *UNCTAD and the North–South Dialogue*.

Chapter 5

1.   Maclagan, *Creation Myths*, p. 48.

2.   Bohm, *Wholeness and the Implicate Order*.

3.   Zukav, *The Dancing Wu Li Masters*, p. 330.

4.   Gale, 'The Anthropic Principle'.

5.   Franz, *Patterns of Creativity Mirrored in Creation Myths*, p. 21.

6.   Coxhead and Miller, *Dreams: Visions of the Night*, p. 1.

7.   Mindell, *Working with the Dreaming Body*.

8.   Mindell, *The Death Walk*.

9.   Franz, op. cit., p. 128.

10. Eliade, *Cosmos and History*, p. 9.

11. Franz, op. cit., pp. 240–41.

12. Maclagan, op. cit., p. 90.

13. Granet, *Das chinesische Denken*.

14. Needham, *Science and Civilisation in China*.

15. Veith (transl.), *The Yellow Emperor's Classic of Internal Medicine*.

16. For further discussion about interacting with the global mind see chapter 12.

Chapter 6

1.   Von Franz, *Creation Myths*, p. 144.

2.   ibid., p. 61.

3.   McLuhan, *Touch the Earth*, p. 119.

4.   Von Franz, op. cit., p. 65–6.

5.   McLuhan, op. cit., p. 15.

6.   Von Franz, op. cit., p. 96.

7.   ibid.

8.   ibid., p. 97.

9.   ibid.

10. ibid., p. 99.

11. Scholem, *On the Kabbalah and its Symbolism* p. 115.

12. The relationship between Adam and the 'fallen sparks' sounds amazingly like the relationship between the solar geomagnetic field and the disturbances,

anxieties and war that are apparently related to this cosmic action. The relationship between our actions on this planet and extraterrestrial phenomena is not just myth. If we *are* influenced by the stars, might not our conflict resolutions affect the solar wind? See Buryl Payne, 'Sunspots and Human Actions' in the Interim Report, May 1986, *Global Peace Meditation Research Project*, pp. 3ff (from the Academy for Peace Research, P O Box 7386 Santa Cruz, California 95060). See also Payne, 'Interaction Between a Human Energy Field and the Geomagnetic Field', *Proceedings of the Gaia Conference*, August 1985. See also H. Ito and A. Bassett, 'Effect of Weak, Pulsing Electromagnetic Fields on Neural Regeneration in the Rat' and F. Playfair and S. Hill, *The Cycles of Heaven*.

Chapter 7

1. Lovelock, *Gaia: A New Look at Life on Earth*.
2. Weinhold 'Geomancy and Tantric Yoga. Alchemical Processes of the Person and the Planet', and Devereux and Thompson, *The Ley Hunter's Companion*, list these events.
3. Jung, 'Synchronicity, an Acausal Connecting Principle', and Peat, *Synchronicity*.
4. Bohm, *Wholeness and the Implicate Order*.
5. Sheldrake, *A New Science of Life: The Hypothesis of Formative Causation*.
6. Pribram, *Languages of the Brain*.
7. See Einstein and Bell's dilemma as described in Capra, *The Turning Point*.
8. Lovelock, op. cit.
9. Russel, in *The Global Brain*, makes a strong argument in favour of Gaia being a living system, since it is a self-organizing system which maintains a high degree of internal order.
10. Miller, in *Living Systems*, details how the critical subsystems of life can be found in all levels of life, from single cells to supranational systems.
11. Russel, op. cit., Table 1, pp. 29–30.
12. Capra, op. cit., p. 280.
13. Capra, ibid., p. 281.
14. Jung mentions in 'Psychic Energy' how each complex or dream figure is a splinter psyche with its own perception. Thus, we can understand not just the part of the person, but the complexes (in the extended sense) of the organizations in which we live as having minds of their own.
15. Capra, op. cit.
16. Mindell, *Working with the Dreaming Body*.

17. Capra, op. cit., p. 290.

18. Capra, ibid., p. 292.

19. Spence, *Myth and Ritual in Dance, Game, and Rhyme*, p. 116.

20. Modern anthropomorphic theories have been discussed by Jose Arguelles, Teilhard de Chardin and Oliver Reiser, to name just a few researchers. Arguelles's work is especially important. In *The Mayan Factor* he defines geomancy as 'the knowledge of the earth as a planet body, a complete living organism whose elemental processes and rhythmic cycles are intimately connected to our own perceptual structures and biological functions . . . As a science, geomancy describes the structure and functions of the planet body earth in relation to the individual body of man, and to the celestial regions, heaven above.'

Pierre Teilhard de Chardin's noosphere is 'the thinking layer formed by the spreading of the zoological human group above (and discontinuously with) the biosphere'. The noosphere refers to the 'probable place and deposition of the thinking element through the universe'. Thus, given the universality of mind or thinking element, according to de Chardin, 'plants with noosphere, far from being a curiosity in nature, would quite simply be the normal and ultimate product of matter carried to its completions'. De Chardin assumes that the noosphere is an 'additional envelope thrown like a very thin but superactive film all around the earth . . .'

Oliver Reiser defined the psi field (1966) as an equivalent of the noosphere integrating the van Allen radiation belts and the genetic code with binary double helix. Reiser posited that the psi field functions in conjunction with the radiation belts, and, like DNA, operates in a double helix manner. The psi field is something like a planetary 'cerebral cortex, the two hemispheres of which somehow correspond to the two halves of the brain in man and their corresponding functions, as well as the two hemispheres of Western (rational) and Eastern (intuitive) thought'.

Chapter 8

1. *Bhagavad-gita*, p. 90.

2. ibid.

3. ibid., p. 91.

4. ibid.

5. McLuhan, *Touch the Earth*, p. 5.

6. ibid., p. 22.

7. Swami Muktananda, *Siddha Meditation*, p. 6.

8. ibid.

9. ibid., p. 11.

10. I experimented with one of my classes to give them direct experience of Shiva and Shakti. You may want to try this experiment as well. All seventy of us began studying our awareness, Shiva, and noticed how and what we saw, felt and heard. Try this for a moment.

Notice whether you are seeing, hearing or feeling. Your seeing and feeling and hearing are Shiva. Now find out what you feel, see or hear. This is Shakti.

Ask yourself what part of you needs to perceive what it is you are noticing. In other words, who is this Shiva who must perceive this particular Shakti? Wake up Shiva!

Though there were many people in the room, only a few aspects of Shiva and of Shakti surfaced. Most people felt (Shiva felt) discomfort in the body (in Shakti).

We could say that Shiva, the universal dreambody in that space and time, was using people in that room as channels to become more sensitive to Shakti, to hurt. The global mind needed to be awakened to the global body's hurt and used us for that purpose. Of course we can also say that all of us are learning to be more sensitive. However valuable this latter mode of thinking may be personally, it diminishes the sense and awesomeness of the collective unconscious, the field and atmosphere, the pain in which we live. If Shiva's perceptions represent the insensitivity we have to the field in which we live, then we can truly tell our global mind, Shiva, to wake up; knowing your feelings could save Shakti's life.

11. *Bhagavad-gita*, p. 92.

Chapter 9

1. Capra, *The Turning Point*, pp. 286–7.

2. In the Prigogine model of non-equilibrium thermodynamics, we find the beginning of this viewpoint. Prigogine, *From Being to Becoming*.

3. Capra, op. cit., p. 287.

4. ibid., p. 287.

5. Mindell, *The Dreambody in Relationships*.

6. Capra, op. cit., p. 287.

7. ibid.

8. ibid.

Chapter 10

1. All process-work terms and their interconnections can be found in the glossary.

2. See Hine, 'The Basic Paradigm' and Lipnack and Stamps, *The Networking Book*.

3. Lipnack and Stamps, op. cit.

4. Hine, op. cit.

5. Lipnack and Stamps, op. cit., p. 162.

6. Private conversation with Jurg Willi.

7. Patel, 'The Technological Transformation of the Third World'.

8. Gerth and Mills, *Character and Social Structure*.

9. Mindell, *The Dreambody in Relationships*.

10. Patel, op. cit.

11. Hine, op. cit.

12. ibid.

13. Michael and Anderson, 'Now That "Progress" No Longer Unites Us', p. 1.

Chapter 11

1. Kaplan, 'The Hidden Dance'.

2. Mindell, *City Shadows*.

Chapter 12

1. This experiment was videotaped, entitled 'Conflict Resolution and World Consciousness', distributed by the Visionary Company, PO Box 730, Haleiwa Hawaii 96712 USA, tel. 808 638 7820.

2. Hannah, *Active Imagination*.

3. In the documentary film, 'Gimme Shelter', a peaceful hippie concert in 1968 turned into a violent nightmare when the Hell's Angels beat up members of the crowd and killed one man, thereby bringing 300,000 people into an aggressive altered state.

4. Bronfenbrenner, 'The Mirror Image in Soviet–American Relations'.

5. Mindell, *The Dreambody in Relationships*.

Chapter 13

1. Corea, *Need for Change*.

2. Dell, 'The Origins of UNCTAD', p. 28.

3. Dell, op. cit., p. 29.

4. ibid.

5. Mindell, *The Dreambody in Relationships*.

6. Trevor-Roper, Foreword to *Larousse Encyclopedia of Modern History*, p. 10.

7. ibid., pp. 206, 207.

8. Toynbee, Foreword to *Larousse Encyclopedia of Ancient and Medieval History*, p. 10.

9. ibid., p. 11.

10. Muller, in Lipnack and Stamps, *Networking*, p. 134.

11. Capra, *The Turning Point*, p. 288.

12. ibid., p. 289.

Glossary

*term has a separate entry in the glossary

acausal: having an unknown cause, connected through meaning

access: the path to a given part or role* of a humon* field*

altered state: any state* having characteristics which are not part of the primary process* of a humon* and which therefore has an unusual and unpredictable nature

anthropos: a personification of the entire universe that often appears in myths about the origin of the world

archetype: Jung's idea of a collective pattern which forms and appears in dreams and fantasies as images that can be found in all cultures and during all times

awareness: the capacity to discover and to use the channel* of perception

channel: perception modality of a humon.* One of many interconnecting modes of perception, all of which together create our total capacity to perceive. Each channel is relatively independent. Humons* use between five and eight channels at any one time

channel switching: the act of consciously or unconsciously moving from one channel* of perception to another in order to broaden awareness*

collective unconscious: Jung's definition of a creative, memory-filled, pattern-filled field* located outside time and space, and which appears in our fantasies, synchronicities* and dreams

conflict resolution: gaining access* to all the different roles* in a field* and allowing them to interact

consciousness: becoming aware of awareness*

disturber: the interrupter of a primary process* focus

double signal: a piece or whole or an unintended message which usually confuses communication

dreamed up: the morphic tendency of a field* to differentiate and create its own parts

entropy: a measure of how much energy is available for work in a given bounded system

field: a vague atmosphere that we sense with our feelings, fantasies and hallucinations, capable of differentiation and interaction between roles★ or parts.

Gaia: the Greek Earth Goddess, used by Lovelock to refer to the world, since it possesses a homeostatic★, anthropomorphic nature

garbage: information★, such as gossip, jealousy, numinous experience and anger which is neglected and thus infests the global field★

global or universal dreambody: a field★ with a non-physical pattern manifesting itself in organic and inorganic events; any system of interconnected channels★; a hologram★ seeking altered states★, wholeness★, the completion of all its processes★ and perceptions. It has typical phases in development in which awareness★ is created through disturbances to the primary process★. It has a timeless, spaceless, mythic quality, and acausal★ symmetrical couplings between events

global consciousness: awareness★ of the many parts and channels in a human being or group; the feeling of supporting not only a side in a conflict, but the overall system; the ability to be strongly emotional and still remember the feeling and vision of the overall picture

global mind: the wisdom of a dreambody which manifests itself in the tendency to produce experiences enriching its own consciousness★; the global mind tends, by and large, to perpetuate its body

Götterdämmerung: the Germanic myth that the gods will end the world through self-destruction and battle

hierarchy: a centralized form of organization with a leadership

hologram: a field★ in which the same pattern appears in the overall picture as well as in parts of the field★ taken independently of one another

homeostatic: the tendency of all humon★ variables to operate together in such a way as to maintain a dynamic equilibrium and relatively steady temperature, weight, colour, identity and personality; a central characteristic of the primary process★

humon: living human system which is connected to other minds, has some degree of mind and a tendency to perceive. It is the indivisible humanlike element of a field★ created together with other humons and the anthropos★

ideology: a belief which gives meaning to life, and filters out information★ which does not fit

information: a combination of signals★ whose meaning may or may not be consciously perceived

information float: neglected, partially completed ideas, feelings, and opinions which are not part of the identified communication network★

intervention: deliberately bringing in awareness★ of a field's★ primary★ and secondary★ processes, which facilitates its unfolding

leadership: any role★ in a global field★ which is required at a given moment to express information★ necessary to the field★

mentate: the tendency of networks★ and systems to form an identity and to have a primary★ and a secondary★ process

morphic field: Sheldrake's idea of a field★ with memory patterns which form physical and mental life

network: an inexactly defined number of people held together by an ideology★ or belief system and having more than one head

noncausal: (see *acausal*)

non-equilibrium: the name of processes★ which occur far from a peaceful state★ and which usually evoke fear and excitement

nonlinear: an indirect relationship between two variables, such as the number of bacteria and the onset of a cold

nonlocality: the principle in physics describing the apparent lack of space between two signals

occupation: the tendency for a field★ to dream up★ people to fill each of its roles★ in order to express itself completely. The people whose natures are closest to a given role★ in a given field★ must fill it

polycephalous: many-headed; a characteristic of a network★ in which there are many different leadership positions

primary process: our common, habitual identity and focus.

process: the flow or exchange of information★; a perceptual matrix; a pattern describing a network★ of interconnecting signals★ and channels★. The total process for a humon★ is a combination of all of its identified and potentially identifiable signals★. When *process* is used as a verb it means enabling the above signal and message flow to occur.

role: one of the necessary parts of the field★ whose interaction creates its atmosphere

secondary process: an unpredictable humon★ focus consisting of a group of signals★ and messages with which the humon★ does not choose to identify itself. The secondary process disturbs the humon's preferred focus and identity

Shakti: the Indian goddess who represents the observed world, perceptions

Shiva: (Siva), the Indian god embodying the act of perception

signal: a momentary, elementary perception in a particular mode or channel★; a piece of information★

SPIN: Virginia Hine's acronym for network★ structures: S = segmented, P = polycephalous★, I = ideology★, and N = network★

SPINAG: a non-equilibrium, process-oriented network★ structure where A (awareness★) and G (garbage★) are added to SPIN★, as defined above

spiritual warrior: a human being who approaches conflict with consciousness★, respect and awe, and with the knowledge that he or she is being dreamed up★ by the global field★ to be a channel★ for this field★

state: the momentary appearance of a process★

static state: a process★ in a state★ which is not changing

synchronicity: Jung's idea of two events which have causal as well as noncausal★ or meaningful explanations

systems theory: the scientific formulation of the network★ structure and evolution of organizations

Tao: the Chinese concept of a field★ to which we must adjust which organizes and patterns the environment

teleology: the philosophy that events are organized by the meaning they have for an observer

trance: a static state★ of awareness★ highly inaccessible to interventions★ because the person in this state does not identify with it

universal dreambody: (see *global dreambody*)

wholeness: the humon★ tendency to become aware of all modes of perception, all inner perceivers and their couplings; the tendency to complete processes★ and the tendency to gain access★ to all parts

world process theatre: a collective drama in which roles★ are filled by given individuals or groups in order to polarize a field★ sufficiently to reconstruct a given atmosphere

xenophobic: fearful of new or unknown events

Bibliography

Adams, Brooks, *The Law of Civilization and Decay*, Freeport, New York, Books for Libraries, 1971.

Arguelles, Jose, *Earth Ascending: An Illustrated Treatise on The Law Governing Whole Systems*, Boulder, Shambhala, 1984.

The Mayan Factor, Santa Fe, Bear & Company, 1987.

Ayres, R., *Banking on the Poor: The World Bank and World Poverty*, Cambridge, Massachusetts, MIT Press, 1983.

Barasch, D., and Lipton, J., *Stop Nuclear War: A Handbook*, New York, Grove, 1982.

Barrett, William, *The Illusion of Technique*, Garden City, New York, Doubleday/Anchor Books, 1978.

Bateson, Gregory, *Mind and Nature*, New York, Dutton, 1979.

Bennet, Steven, J., 'Patterns of the Sky and Earth: the Chinese Science of Applied Cosmology', *Chinese Science*, vol. III, University of Pennsylvania, 1978.

Bentov, Itzhak, *Stalking the Wild Pendulum*, New York, Dutton, 1977.

Bhagavad-gita, with a commentary based on the original sources by R. C. Zaehner, Oxford, Oxford University Press, 1969.

Bohm, David, *Wholeness and the Implicate Order*, London, Routledge & Kegan Paul, 1980.

Bookchin, Murray, *The Limits of the City*, New York, Harper & Row, 1974.

Boulding, Kenneth E., *Ecodynamics: A New Theory of Societal Evolution*, Beverly Hills, California, Sage, 1978.

Boyle, R. H., and Boyle, R. A., *Acid Rain*, New York, Schocken Books, 1983.

Bronfenbrenner, Urie, 'The Mirror Image in Soviet–American Relations', in *Psychology and the Prevention of Nuclear War*, ed. Ralph K. White, New York, New York University Press, 1986, pp. 71–81.

Bugental, J., *Psychotherapy and Process*, New York, Addison-Wesley, 1978.

Capra, F., *The Turning Point*, New York, Simon & Schuster, 1982.

The Tao of Physics, Boulder, Shambhala, 1975.

Carlson, Don, and Comstock, Craig eds., *Securing Our Planet: How to Succeed When Threats are Too Risky and There's Really No Defense*, Los Angeles, J. P. Tarcher, 1986.

eds., *Citizen Summitry*, Los Angeles, J. P. Tarcher, 1986.

Castaneda, Carlos, *Journey to Ixtlan*, New York, Simon & Schuster, 1972.

Tales of Power, New York, Simon & Schuster, 1974.

Center for Defense Information, 'Soviet Geopolitical Momentum: Myth or Menace', *The Defense Monitor*, vol. IX, no. 1, 1980.

Corea, Gamani, *Need for Change*, Oxford, Pergamon Press, 1980.

'UNCTAD: The Changing Scene', in *UNCTAD and the North–South Dialogue*, ed. Michael Zammit Cutajar, Oxford, Pergamon Press, 1985, pp. 295–303.

Council on Environmental Quality, *The Global 2000 Report to the President*, Washington, D C, U S Government Printing Office, 1979.

Coxhead, David, and Hiller, Susan, *Dreams: Visions of the Night*, London, Thames & Hudson, 1978.

Curle, Adam, *Mystics and Militants*, London, Tavistock Publications, 1972.

Cutajar, Zammit Michael, ed., *UNCTAD and the North–South Dialogue*, Oxford, Pergamon Press, 1985.

Daly, Herman E., *Steady-State Economics*, San Francisco, Freeman, 1977.

Davidson, W., 'Psychiatry and Foreign Affairs', *Psychiatric Annals*, 13 (1983), pp. 124–133.

Davies, Paul, *Superforce: The Search for a Grand Unified Theory of Nature*, New York, Simon & Schuster, 1984.

Davis, W. Jackson, *The Seventh Year: Industrial Civilization in Transition*, New York, Norton, 1979.

Dayan, Moshe, *Breakthrough: A Personal Account of the Egypt–Israel Peace Negotiations*, London, Weidenfeld & Nicolson, 1981.

Deane, Phyllis, *The Evolution of Economic Ideas*, London, Cambridge University Press, 1978.

Dell, Sidney, 'The Origins of UNCTAD', in *UNCTAD and the North–South Dialogue*, ed. Michael Zammit Cutajar, Oxford, Pergamon Press, 1985, pp. 10–32.

Deutsch, M., 'The Prevention of World War III: A Psychological Perspective', *Political Psychology*, 4 (1983), pp. 3–31.

Devereux, Paul, and Thomson, I. *Ley Hunters Companion:* Aligned Ancient Sites – A New Study with Field Guide and Maps, London, Thames & Hudson, 1979.

Dolci, Danilo, *The World is One Creature*, translated by Justin Vitiello, New York, Amity House, 1984.

Donati, P. R., 'Organization Between Movement and Institution', *Social Science Information* 24 (1984).

Einstein, A., *On Peace*, London, Methuen, 1963.

Eliade, Mircea, *Cosmos and History*, New York, Harper & Row, 1959.

Fehsenfeld, Thomas, 'On-line with Conflict Management' in *Citizen Summitry*, ed. Don Carlson and Craig Comstock, Los Angeles, J. P. Tarcher, 1986, pp. 355–66.

Feynman, Richard P., 'The Theory of Positrons', *Physical Review*, vol. 76, no. 6 (1949).

Frank, J., *Sanity and Survival in the Nuclear Age: Psychological Aspects of War and Peace*, 2nd edn, New York, Random House, 1982.

Franz, Marie Louise Von, *Patterns of Creativity Mirrored in Creation Myths*, Zurich, Spring, 1972.

Time, Rhythm and Repose, London, Thames & Hudson, 1978.

Gale, George, 'The Anthropic Principle', *Scientific American*, vol. 245 (December 1981), pp. 114–22.

Georgescu-Roegen, Nicholas, 'The Steady State and Ecological Salvation: A Thermodynamic Analysis', *Bioscience*, 27 (April 1977).

Gerlach, L. P. and Hine, V. H., *People, Power, Change: Movements of Social Transformation*, Indianapolis, Bobbs-Merrill, 1970.

Gerth, Hans, and Mills, C. Wright, *Character and Social Structure*, London, Routledge & Kegan Paul, 1954.

Globus, A., and Globus, G., 'The Man of Knowledge', in *Beyond Health and Normality: Explorations of Exceptional Psychological Wellbeing*, ed. R. Walsh and D. H. Shapiro, New York, Van Nostrand Reinhold, 1983, pp. 294–318.

Granet, Marcel, *Das chinesische Denken*, Munich, R. Piper, Verlag, 1963.

Grant, Neil, and Meddleton, Nick, *Atlas of the World Today*, New York, Harper & Row, 1987.

Grof, Stanislav, 'Journeys Beyond the Brain.' (Unpublished manuscript.)

Guerrero, Manuel Perez, 'Collective Self-Reliance: Turning a Concept into a Reality', in *UNCTAD and the North–South Dialogue*, ed. Michael Zammit Cutajar, Oxford, Pergamon Press, 1985, pp. 235–42.

Guntern, Gottlieb, 'Die Kopernikanische Revolution in der Psychotherapie: Wandel vom Psychoanalytischen zum systemischen Paradigma', in *Der familien Mensch: systemisches Denken und Handeln in der Therapie*, ed. Josef Duss-von Werdt and Rosmarie Welter-Enderline, Stuttgart, Klett-Cotta, 1980.

Social Change, Stress and Mental Health in the Pearl of the Alps: A Systematic Study of a Village Process, Berlin, Springer, 1979.

Hannah, Barbara, *Active Imagination*, Boston, Sigo Press, 1982.

Harman, Willis, 'The Coming Transformation', *The Futurist*, 11 (April 1977).

    Global Mind Change. The Promise of the Last Years of the Twentieth Century, Indianapolis, Knowledge Systems Inc., 1988.

Henderson, Hazel, *The Politics of the Solar Age: Alternatives to Economics*, Garden City, New York, Anchor/Doubleday, 1981.

Hersch, S., *The Price of Power*, New York, Summit, 1983.

Hine, Virginia H., 'The Basic Paradigm of a Future Socio-cultural System', Center Report, Center for the Study of Democratic Institutions (1977).

Houston, Jean, 'Prometheus Rebound: An Inquiry into Technological Growth and Psychological Change', in *Alternatives to Growth* vol. I, A Search for Sustainable Futures, ed. Dennis L. Meadows, Cambridge, Massachusetts, Ballinger, 1977.

Hoyle, Fred, and Wickramsinghe, N.C., *Lifecloud: The Origin of Life in the Universe*, New York, Harper & Row, 1979.

Independent Commission on Disarmament and Security Issues, *Common Security: a Programme for Disarmament*, London, Pan Books, 1982.

Ito, H. and Bassett, A., 'Effect of Weak, Pulsing Electromagnetic Fields on Neural Regeneration in the Rat', *Clinical Orthopaedics*, 181 (1983), pp. 283–90.

Janis, Irving L., 'International Crisis Management in the Nuclear Age', in *Psychology and the Prevention of Nuclear War*, ed. Ralph K. White, New York, New York University Press, 1986, pp. 381–96.

Jantsch, Erich, *The Self-organizing Universe*, New York, Pergamon, 1980.

    and Waddington, C. eds., *Evolution and Consciousness: Human Systems in Transition*, Reading, Massachusetts, Addison-Wesley, 1976.

Jung, C. G., 'The Psychogenesis of Mental Disease', in Read, Herbert, Fordham, Michael, and Adler, Gerhard eds., *The Collected Works of Carl G. Jung*, vol. 2, Princeton, Princeton University Press, 1928.

    'On Psychic Energy', *The Collected Works*, vol. 8.

    Mysterium Coniunctionis, *The Collected Works*, vol. 14.

    'Synchronicity, an Acausal Connecting Principle', *The Collected Works*, vol. 16.

    Memories, Dreams and Reflections, New York, Random House/Vintage, 1965.

Kaplan, Amy, 'The Hidden Dance, An Introduction to Process Oriented Movement Work'. (Masters thesis at Antioch University, Yellow Springs, Ohio, 1986.)

Kaplan, Stephen S., *Diplomacy of Power: Soviet Armed Forces as a Political Instrument*, Washington, DC, The Brookings Institution, 1981.

Keegan, John, and Wheatcroft, Andrew, *Zones of Conflict, an Atlas of Future Wars*, London, Jonathan Cape, 1986.

Keen, Samuel, *Faces of the Enemy*, New York, Harper & Row, 1988.

Keleman, Herbert C., 'An Interactional Approach to Conflict Resolution', in *Psychology and the Prevention of Nuclear War*, ed. Ralph K. White, New York, New York University Press, 1986, pp. 171–93.

Kenton, Warren, *Astrology*, London, Thames & Hudson, 1974.

King, Martin Luther, *The Words of Martin Luther King*, selected by Coretta Scott King, New York, Newmarket Press, 1987.

Klapp, Orrin E., *Opening and Closing: Strategies and Information Adaption in Society*, Cambridge, Cambridge University Press, 1978.

Klossowski de Rola, Stanislas, *The Secret Art of Alchemy*, London, Thames & Hudson, 1973.

Koestler, Arthur, *Janus*, London, Hutchinson, 1978.

Kuhn, Thomas S., *The Structure of Scientific Revolutions*, Chicago, University of Chicago Press, 1970.

Larousse Encyclopedia of Ancient and Medieval History, ed. Marcel Dunan, with a foreword by Arnold Toynbee, London, Paul Hamlyn, 1963.

Larousse Encyclopedia of Modern History, ed. Marcel Dunan, with a foreword by Hugh Trevor-Roper, London, Hamlyn, 1968 (Spring Books, 1987).

Lawlor, Robert, *Sacred Geometry*, New York, Crossroads Publishers, 1982.

Lebow, Richard Ned, 'Decision Making in Crises', in *Psychology and the Prevention of Nuclear War*, ed. Ralph K. White, New York, New York University Press, 1986, pp. 397–413.

Leonard, George B., *The Transformation: A Guide to the Inevitable Changes in Humankind*, Los Angeles, J. P. Tarcher, 1981.

Lipnack, Jessica, and Stamps, Jeffrey, *Networking: The First Report and Directory*, New York, Doubleday, 1982.

   The Networking Book: People Connecting with People, London, Routledge & Kegan Paul, 1986.

Loup, J., *Can the Third World Survive?* Baltimore, Johns Hopkins University Press, 1983.

Lovelock, James E., *Gaia: A New Look at Life on Earth*, London and New York, Oxford University Press, 1979.

Maclagan, David, *Creation Myths*, London, Thames & Hudson, 1977.

McLuhan, T. C., *Touch the Earth*, New York, Outerbridge & Dienstfrey, 1971.

Macy, J., *Despair and Personal Power in the Nuclear Age*, Philadelphia, New Society Publishers, 1983.

Marsh, A., *Protest and Political Consciousness*, Beverly Hills, California, Sage, 1977.

Melucci, Alberto, 'The Symbolic Challenge of Contemporary Movements', *Social Research*, vol. 52, no. 4, winter 1985.

Michael, Donald N., and Anderson, Walter Truett, 'Now That "Progress" No Longer Unites Us', *New Options* 33 (24 November 1986), p. 1.

Michell, John, *The New View Over Atlantis*, San Francisco, Harper & Row, 1983.

Miller, James Grier, *Living Systems*, New York, McGraw-Hill, 1978, London, Penguin Books, 1988.

Mindell, Arnold, *City Shadows: Psychological Interventions in Psychiatry*, London and New York, Arkana, 1988.

    Coma, Key to Awakening, Boston, Shambhala, 1989.

    'Conflict Resolution'. (Videotape distributed by Colorado Institute for Conflict Resolution and Creative Leadership (CICRCL), Colorado Springs, Colorado, 1988.)

    The Death Walk. Unpublished manuscript.

    Dreambody, Boston, Sigo Press, 1982; London, Penguin Books, 1988.

    The Dreambody in Relationships, London and New York, Arkana, 1988.

    Inner Dreambodywork: Working with Yourself Alone, London and New York, Arkana, 1989.

    River's Way, London and New York, Arkana, 1988.

    Working with the Dreaming Body, London and New York, Arkana, 1988.

Mitchell, John, *The Earth Spirit: Its Ways, Shrines and Mysteries*, London, Thames & Hudson, 1975.

    A Little History of Astro-Archeology, Great Britain, BAS Printers, 1977.

Muktananda, Swami Paramahansa, *The Play of Consciousness*, California, Shree Gurudev Siddha Yoga Ashram, 1974.

    In the Company of a Siddha. Interviews and Conversations with Swami Muktananda, Ganeshpuri, India, Gurudev Siddha Peeth, 1981.

    Siddha Meditation, Ganeshpuri, Shree Gurudev Ashram, 1975.

Muller, Robert, *Most of All, They Taught me Happiness*, New York, Image Books, 1985.

    New Genesis, Garden City, New York, Image Books/Doubleday, 1984.

Naisbitt, John, *Megatrends*, New York, Warner Books, 1982.

Needham, Joseph, *Science and Civilization in China*, 2 vols., Cambridge, Cambridge University Press, 1954–6.

Neidhardt, John G., *Black Elk Speaks*, Nebraska, University of Nebraska Press, 1961.

Office of Technology Assessment, *The Effects of Nuclear War*, Washington, DC, US Government Printing Office, 1979.

Patel, Surendra J., 'The Technological Transformation of the Third World', in *UNCTAD and the North–South Dialogue*, ed. Michael Zammit Cutajar, Oxford, Pergamon Press, 1985, pp. 124–44.

Payne, Buryl, 'Interim Report', in *Global Peace Meditation and Research Project*, Santa Cruz, California, Academy for Peace Research, May 1986, p. 3.

'Interaction Between a Human Energy Field and the Geomagnetic Field', *Proceedings of the Gaia Conference* (August, 1985).

Peat, David F., *Synchronicity, The Bridge between Matter and Mind*, New York, Bantam Books, 1987.

Peck, M. Scott, *The Different Drum, Community Making and Peace*, New York, Touchstone, 1988.

Pepper, Stephen, *World Hypotheses*, Berkeley, University of California Press, 1942.

Playfair, F., and Hill, S., *The Cycles of Heaven*, New York, Avon, 1978.

Population Reference Bureau, *Annual Report*, Washington, DC, Population Reference Bureau, 1983.

Pribram, Karl, *Languages of the Brain: Experimental Paradoxes and Principles in Neuropsychology*, Englewood Cliffs, New Jersey, Prentice-Hall, 1971.

Prigogine, Ilya, *From Being To Becoming*, San Francisco, Freeman, 1980.

Purce, Jill, *The Mystic Spiral: Journey of the Soul*, London, Thames & Hudson, 1975.

Rawson, Philip, and Legeza, Laszlo, *Tao: The Chinese Philosophy of Time and Change*, London, Thames & Hudson, 1973.

Reid, Howard, and Croucher, Michael, *The Fighting Arts: Great Master of the Martial Arts*, New York, Simon & Schuster, 1983.

Reiser, Oliver, *Cosmic Humanism: A Theory of the Eight Dimensional Cosmos Based on Integrative Principles from Science, Religion and Art*, Cambridge, Mass., Schenkman, 1966.

Rifkin, Jeremy, *Entropy*, New York, Viking, 1980.

Robertson, James, *The Sane Alternative*, St Paul, Minnesota, River Basin Publishing Company, 1979.

Rossen, Stein, 'Global Management of Processes of Change and Adjustment', in *UNCTAD and the North–South Dialogue*, ed. Michael Zammit Cutajar, Oxford, Pergamon Press, 1985, pp. 260–94.

Roszak, Theodore, *Person/Planet*, New York, Doubleday/Anchor, 1978.

Unfinished Animal: The Aquarian Frontier and the Evolution of Consciousness, New York, Harper & Row (Colophon Books), 1977.

Rothstein, Robert L., *Global Bargaining: UNCTAD and the Quest for a New International Economic Order*, Princeton, Princeton University Press, 1979.

Rudhyar, Dane, *The Magic of Tone and the Art of Music*, Boulder, Shambhala, 1982.

Russel, Peter, *The Global Brain: Speculations on the Evolutionary Leap to Planetary Consciousness*, Los Angeles, J. P. Tarcher, 1983.

Sagan, Carl, *The Cosmic Connection*, Garden City, New York, Anchor/Doubleday, 1973.

Samples, Bob, *Mind of Our Mother*, New York, Addison Wesley, 1981.

Satin, Mark, *New Age Politics*, New York, Delta Books, 1979.

Schell, J., *The Fate of the Earth*, New York, Knopf, 1982.

Scholem, Gershom G., *On the Kabbalah and Its Symbolism*, New York, Schocken Books, 1965.

Sharkey, John, *Celtic Mysteries*, London, Thames & Hudson, 1975.

Sheldrake, Rupert, *A New Science of Life: The Hypothesis of Formative Causation*, Los Angeles, J. P. Tarcher, 1982.

'Mind, Memory and Archetype', *Psychological Perspectives*, vol. 18, no. 1, Jung Institute of Los Angeles (spring 1987).

'Extended Mind, Power and Prayer', *Psychological Perspectives*, vol. 19, no. 1 (1988).

Skinner, Stephen, *Terrestrial Astrology: Divination by Geomancy*, London, Routledge & Kegan Paul, 1980, pp. 1–31.

The Living Earth Manual of Feng Shui: Chinese Geomancy, London, Routledge & Kegan Paul, 1982.

Spangler, David, *Towards a Planetary Vision*, Scotland, The Findhorn Press, 1978.

Spence, Lewis, *Myth and Ritual in Dance, Game and Rhyme*, London, Watts, 1947.

Tarrow, S., 'Struggling to Reform: Social Movements and Policy Change During Cycles of Protest', *Western Societies Occasional Papers* 15, Ithaca, NY, Cornell University, 1983.

Teilhard de Chardin, Pierre, *The Phenomenon of Man*, New York, Harper & Row, 1965.

Thomas, Lewis, *The Lives of a Cell*, New York, Bantam, 1975.

Thompson, William Irwin, *From Nation to Emanation, Planetary Culture and World Governance*, Scotland, The Findhorn Press, 1982.

Tompkins, Peter, and Bird, Christopher, *The Secret Life of Plants*, New York, Harper & Row, 1973.

Toynbee, Arnold, *A Study of History*, New York, Oxford University Press, 1934.

Wainhouse, David, *International Peace Observation, A History and Forecast*, Baltimore and London, Johns Hopkins University Press, 1969.

Walsh, Roger, *Staying Alive*, Boulder, Shambhala, 1984.

Watson, Lyall, *Lifetide*, London, Hodder & Stoughton, 1979.

Webb, K., *et al.*, 'Etiology and Outcomes of Protest: New European Perspectives', *American Behavioral Scientist*, 26, no. 3 (1983).

Weinhold, Janae, 'Geomancy and Tantric Yoga, Alchemical Processes of the Person and the Planet', Unpublished manuscript.

Weiss, Thomas G., *Multilateral Development Diplomacy in UNCTAD, The Lessons of Group Negotiations, 1964–84*, New York, Macmillan, 1986.

White, Ralph K., ed., *Psychology and the Prevention of Nuclear War*, New York, New York University Press, 1986.

Wilber, K. ed., *Quantum Questions: The Mystical Writings of the Great Physicists*, Boulder, Shambhala (New Science Library), 1984.

Wilhelm, Richard, *The I Ching*, London, Routledge & Kegan Paul, 1968.

Wright, Quincy, *A Study of War*, London, University of Chicago Press, 1967.
The Yellow Emperor's Classic of Internal Medicine, translated by Ilza Veith, Berkeley, University of California Press, 1966.

Zacher, Mark W., 'International Conflicts and Collective Security 1946–77', New York, Praeger Special Studies), 1979.

Zukav, Gary, *The Dancing Wu Li Masters*, New York, William Morrow, 1979.

ARKANA – NEW-AGE BOOKS FOR MIND, BODY AND SPIRIT

With over 150 titles currently in print, Arkana is the leading name in quality new-age books for mind, body and spirit. Arkana encompasses the spirituality of both East and West, ancient and new, in fiction and non-fiction. A vast range of interests are covered, including Psychology and Transformation, Health, Science and Mysticism, Women's Spirituality and Astrology.

If you would like a catalogue of Arkana books, please write to:

Arkana Marketing Department
Penguin Books Ltd
27 Wright's Lane
London W8 5TZ

ARKANA – NEW-AGE BOOKS FOR MIND, BODY AND SPIRIT

A selection of titles already published or in preparation

On Having No Head: Zen and the Re-Discovery of the Obvious
D. E. Harding

'Reason and imagination and all mental chatter died down . . . I forgot my name, my humanness, my thingness, all that could be called me or mine. Past and future dropped away . . .'

Thus Douglas Harding describes his first experience of headlessness, or no self. This classic work truly conveys the experience that mystics of all ages have tried to put into words.

Self-Healing: My Life and Vision   Meir Schneider

Born blind, pronounced incurable – yet at 17 Meir Schneider discovered self-healing techniques which within four years led him to gain a remarkable degree of vision. In the process he discovered an entirely new self-healing system, and an inspirational faith and enthusiasm that helped others heal themselves. While individual response to self-healing is unique, the healing power is inherent in all of us.

'This remarkable story is tonic for everyone who believes in the creative power of the human will' – Marilyn Ferguson.

The Way of the Craftsman: A Search for the Spiritual Essence of Craft Freemasonry   W. Kirk MacNulty

This revolutionary book uncovers the Kabbalistic roots of Freemasonry, showing how Kabbalistic symbolism informs all of its central rituals. W. Kirk MacNulty, a Freemason for twenty-five years, reveals how the symbolic structure of the Craft is designed to lead the individual step by step to psychological self-knowledge, while at the same time recognising mankind's fundamental dependence on God.

Dictionary of Astrology   Fred Gettings

Easily accessible yet sufficiently detailed to serve the needs of the practical astrologer, this fascinating reference book offers reliable definitions and clarifications of over 3000 astrological terms, from the post-medieval era to today's most recent developments.

ARKANA – NEW-AGE BOOKS FOR MIND, BODY AND SPIRIT

A selection of titles already published or in preparation

The I Ching and You Diana ffarington Hook

A clear, accessible, step-by-step guide to the *I Ching* – the classic book of Chinese wisdom. Ideal for the reader seeking a quick guide to its fundamental principles, and the often highly subtle shades of meaning of its eight trigrams and sixty-four hexagrams.

A History of Yoga Vivian Worthington

The first of its kind, *A History of Yoga* chronicles the uplifting teachings of this ancient art in its many guises: at its most simple a beneficial exercise; at its purest an all-embracing quest for the union of body and mind.

Tao Te Ching The Richard Wilhelm Edition

Encompassing philosophical speculation and mystical reflection, the *Tao Te Ching* has been translated more often than any other book except the Bible, and more analysed than any other Chinese classic. Richard Wilhelm's acclaimed 1910 translation is here made available in English.

The Book of the Dead E. A. Wallis Budge

Intended to give the deceased immortality, the Ancient Egyptian *Book of the Dead* was a vital piece of 'luggage' on the soul's journey to the other world, providing for every need: victory over enemies, the procurement of friendship and – ultimately – entry into the kingdom of Osiris.

Yoga: Immortality and Freedom Mircea Eliade

Eliade's excellent volume explores the tradition of yoga with exceptional directness and detail.

'One of the most important and exhaustive single-volume studies of the major ascetic techniques of India and their history yet to appear in English' – *San Francisco Chronicle*

ARKANA – NEW-AGE BOOKS FOR MIND, BODY AND SPIRIT

A selection of titles already published or in preparation

Neal's Yard Natural Remedies Susan Curtis, Romy Fraser and Irene Kohler

Natural remedies for common ailments from the pioneering Neal's Yard Apothecary Shop. An invaluable resource for everyone wishing to take responsibility for their own health, enabling you to make your own choice from homeopathy, aromatherapy and herbalism.

The Arkana Dictionary of New Perspectives Stuart Holroyd

Clear, comprehensive and compact, this iconoclastic reference guide brings together the orthodox and the highly unorthodox, doing full justice to *every* facet of contemporary thought – psychology and parapsychology, culture and counter-culture, science and so-called pseudo-science.

The Absent Father: Crisis and Creativity Alix Pirani

Freud used Oedipus to explain human nature; but Alix Pirani believes that the myth of Danae and Perseus has most to teach an age which offers 'new responsibilities for women and challenging questions for men' – a myth which can help us face the darker side of our personalities and break the patterns inherited from our parents.

Woman Awake: A Celebration of Women's Wisdom Christina Feldman

In this inspiring book, Christina Feldman suggests that it *is* possible to break out of those negative patterns instilled into us by our social conditioning as women: confirmity, passivity and surrender of self. Through a growing awareness of the dignity of all life and its connection with us, we can regain our sense of power and worth.

Water and Sexuality Michel Odent

Taking as his starting point his world-famous work on underwater childbirth at Pithiviers, Michel Odent considers the meaning and importance of water as a symbol: in the past – expressed through myths and legends – and today, from an advertisers' tool to a metaphor for aspects of the psyche. Dr Odent also boldly suggests that the human species may have had an aquatic past.

ARKANA – NEW-AGE BOOKS FOR MIND, BODY AND SPIRIT

A selection of titles already published or in preparation

Encyclopedia of the Unexplained
Edited by Richard Cavendish   Consultant: J. B. Rhine

'Will probably be the definitive work of its kind for a long time to come' – *Prediction*

The ultimate guide to the unknown, the esoteric and the unproven: richly illustrated, with almost 450 clear and lively entries from Alchemy, the Black Box and Crowley to faculty X, Yoga and the Zodiac.

Buddhist Civilization in Tibet   Tulku Thondup Rinpoche

Unique among works in English, *Buddhist Civilization in Tibet* provides an astonishing wealth of information on the various strands of Tibetan religion and literature in a single compact volume, focusing predominantly on the four major schools of Buddhism: Nyingma, Kagyud, Sakya and Gelug.

The Living Earth Manual of Feng-Shui   Stephen Skinner

The ancient Chinese art of Feng-Shui – tracking the hidden energy flow which runs through the earth in order to derive maximum benefit from being in the right place at the right time – can be applied equally to the siting and layout of cities, houses, tombs and even flats and bedsits; and can be practised as successfully in the West as in the East with the aid of this accessible manual.

In Search of the Miraculous: Fragments of an Unknown Teaching   P. D. Ouspensky

Ouspensky's renowned, vivid and characteristically honest account of his work with Gurdjieff from 1915–18.

'Undoubtedly a *tour de force*. To put entirely new and very complex cosmology and psychology into fewer than 400 pages, and to do this with a simplicity and vividness that makes the book accessible to any educated reader, is in itself something of an achievement' – *The Times Literary Supplement*

ARKANA – NEW-AGE BOOKS FOR MIND, BODY AND SPIRIT

A selection of titles already published or in preparation

The Ghost in the Machine Arthur Koestler

Koestler's classic work – which can be read alone or as the conclusion of his trilogy on the human mind – is concerned not with human creativity but with human pathology.

'He has seldom been as impressive, as scientifically far-ranging, as lively-minded or as alarming as on the present occasion' – John Raymond in the *Financial Times*.

T'ai Chi Ch'uan and Meditation Da Liu

Today T'ai Chi Ch'uan is known primarily as a martial art – but it was originally developed as a complement to meditation. Both disciplines involve alignment of the self with the Tao, the ultimate reality of the universe. Da Liu shows how to combine T'ai Chi Ch'uan and meditation, balancing the physical and spiritual aspects to attain good health and harmony with the universe.

Return of the Goddess Edward C. Whitmont

Amidst social upheaval and the questioning of traditional gender roles, a new myth is arising: the myth of the ancient Goddess who once ruled earth and heaven before the advent of patriarchy and patriachal religion. Here one of the world's leading Jungian analysts argues that our society, long dominated by male concepts of power and aggression, is today experiencing a resurgence of the feminine.

The Strange Life of Ivan Osokin P. D. Ouspensky

If you had the chance to live your life again, what would you do with it? Ouspensky's novel, set in Moscow, on a country estate and in Paris, tells what happens to Ivan Ososkin when he is sent back twelve years to his stormy schooldays, early manhood and early loves. First published in 1947, the *Manchester Guardian* praised it as 'a brilliant fantasy . . . written to illustrate the theme that we do not live life but that life lives us'.

ARKANA – NEW-AGE BOOKS FOR MIND, BODY AND SPIRIT

A selection of titles already published or in preparation

Head Off Stress: Beyond the Bottom Line D. E. Harding

Learning to head off stress takes no time at all and is impossible to forget – all it requires is that we dare take a fresh look at ourselves. This infallible and revolutionary guide from the author of *On Having No Head* – whose work C. S. Lewis described as 'highest genius' – shows how.

Shiatzu: Japanese Finger Pressure for Energy, Sexual Vitality and Relief from Tension and Pain
Yukiko Irwin with James Wagenvoord

The product of 4000 years of Oriental medicine and philosophy, Shiatzu is a Japanese variant of the Chinese practice of acupuncture. Fingers, thumbs and palms are applied to the 657 pressure points that the Chinese penetrate with gold and silver needles, aiming to maintain health, increase vitality and promote well-being.

The Magus of Strovolos: The Extraordinary World of a Spiritual Healer Kyriacos C. Markides

This vivid account introduces us to the rich and intricate world of Daskalos, the Magus of Strovolos – a true healer who draws upon a seemingly limitless mixture of esoteric teachings, psychology, reincarnation, demonology, cosmology and mysticism, from both East and West.

'This is a really marvellous book . . . one of the most extraordinary accounts of a "magical" personality since Ouspensky's account of Gurdjieff' – Colin Wilson

Meetings With Remarkable Men G. I. Gurdjieff

All that we know of the early life of Gurdjieff – one of the great spiritual masters of this century – is contained within these colourful and profound tales of adventure. The men who influenced his formative years had no claim to fame in the conventional sense; what made them remarkable was the consuming desire they all shared to understand the deepest mysteries of life.